freee
baking

freee
baking

100 Favourite
Gluten Free Recipes

Clare Marriage

EBURY
PRESS

Contents

Yorkshire Puddings, Pancakes & Doughnuts

Pastry, Crumbles & Puddings

Pizza, Dumplings & Pasta

Gluten free baking for 50 years!

My gluten free journey of discovery began in the seventies when my mother was advised to follow a gluten free diet. At the time, gluten free living looked very different to how it does now, and free from products were nowhere to be found in our local shops. Unsurprisingly, mealtimes became a real challenge. After all, don't we all want to tuck into delicious food without worrying if it is safe to eat?

Above all, my mother missed bread and cakes, so out of necessity I took my love of baking and began to experiment with naturally gluten free grains and flours to learn if and how, these could be used to make gluten free bakes that were also tasty. I started out baking with individual flours made from grains such as maize and rice. Aside from everything ending up tasting similar and ultimately a little boring using one grain all the time, I soon realised that for some bakes even better results could be achieved by blending different gluten free ingredients together. Over time, the idea formed that perhaps it was possible to create gluten free versions of standard gluten-containing flours such as plain, self-raising and even bread flours.

As I developed more recipes, my own family became my harshest critics. There were many moments of teatime judgement, when I waited for the unanimous sounds of enjoyment from around the kitchen table, which would indicate the success of a recipe. I would regularly go back to the drawing board, to rewrite and re-bake recipes until everyone was happily tucking into brownies, pancakes, pizza and much more – often without even realising they were gluten free.

My very first gluten free flour blend was launched in 2002 and was actually designed to work for all kinds of gluten free baking. However, once this first gluten free flour blend was created, more would follow, as I perfected blending the right quantities of naturally gluten free flours to create different plain, self raising, white and brown bread flours. Ultimately, this range now allows anyone to bake practically anything gluten free, and while today there are many more ready-made gluten free products available to buy than 50 years ago, I think most will agree, there are few things better than serving up something homemade.

This book is aimed at giving you all the tools, tips and recipes you need to be a successful gluten free baker. I've collected my favourite recipes from everyday basics to celebration cakes and I will show you how to make them all in simple steps. Developed, tested and re-tested countless times over many years, including by our customers, I know they deliver great results, every time. My belief has always been that gluten free baking should be no harder than and just as delicious as regular baking and I am confident with this book anyone will be able to experience the joy and pleasures of home-baking and cooking, even if they are gluten free. Happy baking!

CLARE MARRIAGE

Gluten free baking ingredients guide

There are many naturally gluten free ingredients which can be used in gluten free baking. Some will be familiar, but others are perhaps new to you. Discovering and experimenting with different grains and pulses is one of my personal passions and an endless source of joy. It's incredible just how much you can vary the taste and texture of bakes by simply altering the ingredients used. You can make flour from almost anything, so it would be too much to include a full list of ingredients you may encounter on your gluten free baking journey. However, below are some of the more common ingredients that you will find in regular supermarkets or health-food stores. And don't worry, most of the recipes in this book use our pre-made flour blends, so there is no immediate need to go out and buy all these different ingredients to get started!

BUCKWHEAT
Having no relationship or connection with wheat, the triangular buckwheat seed is referred to as a grain although it is in fact a seed from a member of the rhubarb family. After removing the inedible outer husk, buckwheat mills into a lightly speckled flour with a mild, sweet flavour and is sometimes known as sarrasin flour. It is traditionally used to make blinis, galettes and breakfast pancakes, as well as noodles.

CHICKPEA
Popular in Mediterranean, Middle Eastern and Indian cuisine, chickpeas are also known as garbanzo beans. They are a pulse rather than a grain, and are naturally high in protein and in fibre. Pale-yellow chickpea flour is great for sauces, batter and as an egg replacement for those on plant-based diets.

CORNFLOUR
Sometimes called cornstarch, cornflour is a multipurpose thickener which is best for recipes that will be eaten immediately, as sauces thickened with cornflour can be difficult to reheat. Cornflour is the starchy part of maize that thickens boiling liquid into an opaque sauce.

GRAM
Gram flour, or besan, is milled from yellow split peas that are slightly smaller than chickpeas and are known as chana dal in India. Gram flour is a popular ingredient in Indian dishes such as onion bhajis or dosa pancakes and sweat treats such as pistachio fudge. It can also be used in place of eggs in dishes such as omelettes or quiches. High in protein and in fibre, this flour is also surprisingly good for making pastry.

MAIZE OR CORN
Specific varieties of maize, which are also called corn, are grown depending on how they are to be processed and consumed. Some are more suitable for eating as sweetcorn, for making into popcorn, or for milling into flour. Very fine white maize flour can be found in our own cornflour.

OATS

Oats are amongst the oldest grains recorded and remain as popular as ever. They are naturally gluten free but are often grown, transported or processed with wheat, barley and rye. Therefore it's important to always buy specifically gluten free oats. After the inedible outer oat husk has been removed, the oat grain is typically rolled into flakes, which are naturally high in fibre. We use oats in many of our finished products. Oats are also milled into creamy-white, wholegrain oat flour, which has a subtle sweetness and is a versatile ingredient for making crumbles, cookies and muffins.

POTATO

Potatoes are the tubers produced on the roots of the potato plant. Originating in South America, potatoes are now cultivated in many parts of the world. Soft and white, starchy potato flour, sometimes known as fécule, is especially good for thickening soups and stews because it becomes transparent when cooked and does not leave a starchy flavour. It is also good for making a light crisp batter and will even bake into a very light layer cake.

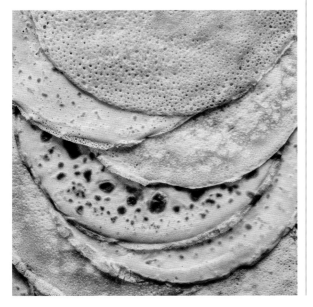

RICE

Rice, of which there are many types, can grow in a variety of conditions, making it a staple grain for many cultures around the world. It has a neutral taste and is easy to digest, so often chosen by those with a delicate digestive system. Off-white and slightly creamy in colour, rice flour can be used in sweet and savoury dishes, for thickening sauces, making pastry, as well as baking cookies and even gluten free bread.

TAPIOCA

This flour is made from the root of the cassava or manioc plant. Naturally white in colour, tapioca is soft and silky with starchy properties that are perfect for making glossy, sweet and savoury items such as chocolate mousse, or sweet chilli sauce. A fine flour, it also makes fantastic tempura batter and light and crispy snap biscuits.

TEFF

One of the world's smallest grains, teff thrives in hot arid climates and is a traditional food in Ethiopia. Technically, teff is a grass rather than a grain and is often referred to as a pseudo cereal. Wholegrain teff flour is off-white in colour, wholesome in flavour, has a good level of protein and is high in fibre.

COCONUT

Coconuts are the fruiting seeds of the coconut palm, which grows mainly in the tropics. The white inner flesh of coconuts is dried and pressed before being ground into coconut flour. This unique alternative to wheat flour is high in fibre and protein, low-carb and naturally gluten free. Full of flavour, we've found it's great for making cakes, cookies, pastry and more.

QUINOA

Originating in South America, quinoa was highly prized by the Inca civilisation. This ancient grain thrives in harsh conditions and climates, producing small grains on colourful red-golden seed heads. Quinoa mills into an off-white flour with a warm, earthy, wholesome flavour. It is a source of fibre and protein that can be used for sweet and savoury baking such as pizza bases.

AMARANTH

Another pseudo-cereal, amaranth, similar to quinoa, originates from the ancient Aztec and Inca civilisations and is a naturally gluten free grain with high protein and fibre levels. It's useful for making unleavened flatbreads like tortillas and chapatis but can also be used in other baking, on its own or mixed with other flours.

SORGHUM

Belonging to the grass family, sorghum has been cultivated for thousands of years and is thought to have originated in Africa. It's drought resistant and popular to grow in drier parts of the world. Finely ground from the wholegrain kernel, sorghum flour has a mild, sweet flavour and works well in many sweet and savoury dishes.

ALMONDS

Almond flour is typically ground from blanched (skinless) almonds, making it light in colour and fine in texture. Low in carbs and high in protein, its high oil content helps make cakes soft and moist. More commonly available and also often used in baking, are ground almonds, which are simply ground, skin-on, unpeeled almonds.

MILLET

Millet is an ancient grain with a nutty flavour and light fluffy texture that works best when combined with other flours for gluten free baking but is also often cooked into a simple porridge. High in fibre and protein, it's known for its nutritional benefits as well as being gluten free. Another grain belonging to the grass family, it originated in Asia and as it is a hardy crop remains a staple in many warmer climates.

FREEE gluten free flour blends

Over the years we have created a core range of flours which helps make gluten free baking as simple and easy as possible. All are made from naturally gluten free ingredients and having these flours in your cupboard means you can bake pretty much anything gluten free.

GLUTEN FREE PLAIN FLOUR

This is the foundation flour to much gluten free baking and a store cupboard favourite. Used for anything from cakes to cookies, pastry to pancakes, scones, biscuits, dumplings and so much more, our special flour blend milled from naturally gluten free ingredients is a great alternative to everyday plain wheat flour. Follow one of our gluten free recipes or adapt a traditional recipe by adding a little extra liquid.

GLUTEN FREE SELF RAISING FLOUR

Another essential store cupboard ingredient, this gluten free self raising flour is an excellent alternative to self raising wheat-based flour. It is made from a special blend of naturally gluten free ingredients with added raising agents. Replace the standard self raising flour in a regular recipe and add a little extra liquid or simply use as instructed if called for in one of our bespoke gluten free recipes.

GLUTEN FREE WHITE BREAD FLOUR

Blended from naturally gluten free ingredients, use this flour as an alternative to white bread flour made from wheat. Gluten free bread is quite different to make compared to regular bread, but using this flour and its associated recipes ensures perfect results every time. Great for white bread loaves, pizza bases, baguettes, ciabatta and even crumpets. Simply follow our recipes to make bread in your oven or bread machine.

GLUTEN FREE BROWN BREAD FLOUR

This flour is a source of fibre and is blended from naturally gluten free ingredients such as rice, gram and buckwheat. Follow our recipes to make tasty brown loaves, rolls and even Christmas puddings with this flour. Also suitable for using in bread machines.

Other helpful ingredients for gluten free baking

Below are a few other ingredients that you'll most likely come across in your gluten free baking. These are naturally gluten free but do make sure you check the label before you use them.

XANTHAN GUM

Xanthan gum is the gluten free baker's best friend. It's made from a sugar created during the fermentation of grain, typically maize, with the bacterium *Xanthomonas campestris*. Gluten is what helps give bread its elasticity and cake crumb its structure, but it's missing in gluten free flours. To solve this, bread and cake crumb can be strengthened by blending xanthan gum with gluten free flour before baking. Most of our flour blends already contain xanthan gum, so there is no need to add it unless it's called for in the recipe.

BAKING POWDER

Baking powder is used to raise many baked items through an acid and alkali reaction that takes place when it is combined with liquid and heat, generating air bubbles and lift during baking. Watch your quantities, though, as when too much baking powder is used, baked goods can taste soapy. You can make your own self raising flour by adding 2 teaspoons of baking powder to 100g of plain white flour.

BICARBONATE OF SODA

Bicarbonate of soda, also known as bicarb and baking soda, is used to raise or aerate many baked items. It is naturally alkaline and combines with the acidic ingredients, such as lemon juice, vinegar or yoghurt used in a recipe, together with oven heat, to generate bubbles and lift during baking. If used in excess it can impart a metallic taste, so only use the recommended amount.

Getting Started

Everything you need to know to make great gluten free breads, cakes, pastry and sauces.

Kitchen notes – allergens & baking equipment

DIETARY INFORMATION

It was my mother's gluten intolerance that set me off on my gluten free journey back in the seventies. Since then, the prevalence of food intolerances and allergies seem to have increased exponentially with many more people affected today than ever before.

With this in mind, my baking, cooking and development of the broader FREEE product range have always aimed to cater not only for those needing to avoid gluten, but often other common allergens such as nuts, eggs and milk too. In this book, I have added colour coded keys to all recipes to help navigate these allergens and on occasion, I have suggested some ingredient swaps to help make my recipes as accessible as possible.

Regarding gluten, people avoid it for different reasons. At one end of the scale, some simply feel better reducing their gluten intake. For others, like those medically diagnosed with coeliac disease, they must follow a gluten free diet always and for life. Regardless of need, I'm very proud to be able to support everyone in a small way with tasty and nutritious gluten free food through this book and the broader FREEE offer.

Finally, remember whenever you cater for anyone who cannot have certain ingredients, make sure everything is cleaned properly before use, you keep utensils, chopping boards, bowls etc apart from anything with the allergen to be avoided, and you stay focused to avoid accidently mixing things up. And of course, always check labels for everything including the alibi labelling (may contain).

ALLERGEN KEY

g **FREE FROM Gluten**
A type of protein found in wheat and other cereals, gluten is known for its ability to develop crumb structure in bread making and create the firmness in pasta. All recipes in this book are gluten free.

e **FREE FROM Egg**
Whole egg, egg yolks and egg white are not used in these recipes. Some excellent gram flour swaps are shown for some recipes.

m **FREE FROM Milk**
Recipes avoiding milk, cream and butter from cows or goats. Plant milk alternatives can be used in most recipes.

n **FREE FROM Peanuts/Nuts**
These recipes do not use nuts including peanuts, almonds, walnuts, pecans, hazelnut or brazil nuts. You may find coconuts or pine nuts in some of these recipes.

IMPORTANT BAKING EQUIPMENT

- **Weighing scales** for accurate measuring of ingredients. Note 1 litre of water weighs 1kg.

- **Measuring spoons, teaspoons and tablespoons** of ingredients should always be level.

- **Sift** together dry ingredients for thorough mixing and best baking results.

- **Wire racks** or a **spare oven shelf** are used for cooling bakes.

- **Bowls** are used for mixing ingredients, but any clean pan or container can be used.

- **Whisks, electric beaters** or a **fork** are used for mixing and beating ingredients.

- **Baking liners** are a reusable, easy-to-clean option for lining baking tins and trays.

BREAD BAKING TINS

These rectangular tins create the loaf shape for bread and are typically referred to as being suitable for a 450g/1lb or 900g/2lb loaf, although sizing can vary enormously. You can also bake bread in a silicone mould, a cast-iron casserole, a clean metal container or Pyrex dish.

We tested the recipes in this book in bread tins measuring;

450g/1lb tin	16 x 10.5cm/6.25 x 4.13 inch
900g/2lb tin	23 x 13cm/9 x 5 inch

BAKING AND OVEN TRAYS

These are ideal for baking small cakes and tarts, individual items and biscuits. Some recipes specify a tray measuring 23 x 13cm/9 x 5 inch which is often referred to as a Swiss roll tray. Cake, muffin and tart trays have varying sizes of holes for these bakes. See also Cake Tin Size Conversion Table on page 237.

Getting started – some fundamentals about gluten free baking

If you're new to gluten free baking, you probably have lots of questions. What's different and what's the same compared to conventional baking? Will gluten free flour work in the same way as regular flour? What flour should I use for different types of bakes? Can you even make bread without gluten-containing flour?

It's true that many of the familiar baking rules are rewritten when baking without conventional wheat flour. The good news is that nowadays gluten free baking is a lot easier than many people think and the results are most often so good you wouldn't even know you were eating something gluten free.

I always recommend using a specific gluten free recipe rather than just swapping in gluten free flour for ordinary flour. This is the approach taken in this book and is the simplest way to achieve a delicious result every time. If you are trying to use gluten free flour in a conventional wheat recipe, it's likely you'll need to add extra liquid, which is possible but can be harder to judge and get just right and may affect the quality of the bake. It is also not possible to make bread using conventional recipes, but the gluten free method is to some extent actually easier and requires no kneading, which is an added benefit for many!

Over the next pages, we'll guide you through all the essentials to give you the basic knowledge and set you off on your gluten free baking journey. The bakes we have picked for this book can be the ones you often miss the most when following a gluten free diet. Once you've mastered these, you'll feel confident trying more challenging recipes, and then the world is your oyster.

Cake fundamentals & basic recipes

You can make wonderful versions of almost any type of cake for any occasion, from small to large, traybake and layer cakes to celebration bakes, using gluten free plain and self-raising flours. However, certain cakes are best made with plain flour while others are best made with bread flour. We recommend you follow a cake recipe that specifies gluten free flour and the resulting bake is likely to be indistinguishable from a conventional cake.

Our top tips for success are:

- If following your own recipe, you will probably need to add extra liquid.

- Preheat your oven 20 minutes before you want to bake.

- To check if your cake is cooked, press a cocktail stick into the middle and if it comes out clean it is cooked.

- Gluten free cakes benefit from some cooling in their tins before turning out to cool thoroughly.

A variety of different cake-mixing methods are typically used for different types of traybakes, small and large cakes. The combining of different sugars and types of flour with different raising agents creates a huge variety of cake types and textures.

A **Creamed Cake**, like a Madeira Loaf Cake (page 58) or Lemon Drizzle Loaf Cake (page 56), starts with a thorough mixing of butter and sugar, known as creaming, followed by the addition of other ingredients and flavourings.

All-in-One Cakes, such as a Victoria Sponge (page 34), assemble all or most of the ingredients into the mixing bowl before thorough mixing and tipping into a cake tin.

A **Boiled Cake** refers to dried fruit that has been gently simmered and added to the cake mixture prior to baking.

The **Melting Method** warms together sugar, syrup and butter or oil to create a viscous liquid, followed by the addition of dry ingredients as in Gingerbread People (page 96) and Flapjacks (page 108).

In the **Whisking Method** eggs and sugar are beaten together until light and fluffy before the addition of further ingredients, as in a Swiss Roll (page 75) or Yule Log (page 76).

Yeasted Cakes are raised with yeast rather than baking powder.

CHOOSING CAKE INGREDIENTS

- Our gluten free flour blends are designed for and tested on cake recipes.

- For best results, use dairy butter or plant butter.

- Our cake recipes are tested using mixed size eggs, so use whichever size you have available.

MIXING CAKE INGREDIENTS

- Blend and sift together the dry ingredients to ensure even distribution.

- Chop the butter or plant butter into small cubes before adding it to the sugar.

- Add a little extra liquid if following a conventional cake recipe to hydrate the flour.

- Beat well after the addition of each egg to prevent curdling.

- Add a spoon of flour to stabilise the cake mixture if it starts to split.

PREPARING BAKING TINS AND TRAYS

- Reusable coated fabric or silicone baking mats, greaseproof paper and baking parchment can be used to line baking tins, or rub the inside of tins and trays with butter or oil.

- After baking, soak tins, trays and reusable liners in hot water with mild soap.

BAKING GLUTEN FREE CAKES

- Always preheat your oven 20 minutes before you are going to bake.

- Look through the oven glass to see how your cake is cooking rather than opening the oven door, which will lower the oven temperature.

- To check if your cake is cooked, press a cocktail stick into the middle. If it comes out clean, the cake is ready.

COOLING CAKES

- Some gluten free cakes can be fragile until cold, so part or all of their cooling should be in the tin.

- Once out of the tin, allow a cake to finish cooling on a wire rack.

STORING CAKE

- Wrap the cold cake in kitchen foil or store in an airtight tin.

- Open-freeze (freeze unwrapped) small cakes and slices of large cake, then wrap and freeze for up to three months.

- Wrap un-iced cake layers individually in kitchen foil before freezing for up to three months.

USING LEFTOVER CAKE

- Break the cake into crumbs and add it to a crumble topping.

- Cake crumbs can be used instead of breadcrumbs in Treacle Tart (page 191).

- Slice and open-freeze large cakes, then wrap and freeze for up to three months.

Bread fundamentals
& basic recipes

A home-baked loaf can be a real treat and for many it is their preferred choice over shop-bought bread. This allows you to avoid certain processing aids as well as being more economical.

Conventional bread recipes are not suited to gluten free baking but there is a wide choice of gluten free breads that can be made in the oven, an air fryer or bread machine.

As gluten free bread is best eaten on the day of baking, we recommend slicing, wrapping and freezing slices to enjoy on another day. Day-old bread can be refreshed by popping it in a toaster or crumbling it into breadcrumbs, which will freeze well.

Conventional bread baking develops the naturally occurring gluten present in wheat through kneading the dough to create the crumb structure of a loaf. As there is no gluten in white, brown or seeded gluten free flours, conventional bread-making rules must be adapted to create equally delicious loaves. Home-baked gluten free bread is mostly made using a batter rather than a dough and, as there is no gluten in the flour, kneading is not necessary. You can also bake delicious gluten free sourdough bread. Gluten free flour can also be used to make many other styles of bread such as Flatbreads (page 124), Naan (page 125), Baguettes (page 126) and Ciabatta (page 133).

Our top tips for success are:

- Follow a gluten free bread recipe, without omitting or substituting ingredients.

- Preheat your oven 20 minutes before you want to bake.

- Make sure gluten free bread is cold before slicing.

Bread Baking Using a Bread Machine

Offering an easy and convenient way to bake, a machine loaf can go a long way if sliced and frozen for later use. Always check the quantities of your chosen recipe are suitable for your bread machine. To check your bread pan size with recipe quantities, see the chart below. Measure the volume of your bread pan by standing it on scales and filling it with water, noting that 1kg is equal to 1 litre. Compare the small, medium and large pan volumes with corresponding recipe quantities.

Small	Medium	Large
1.9 litre (1.9kg) pan volume	2.4 litre (2.4kg) pan volume	3 litre (3kg) pan volume
1½-2lb/700g-900g loaf	2-2½lb/900g-1.2kg loaf	2½-3lb/1.2-1.7kg loaf
8-10 slices	12-14 slices	14-16 slices

If your bread machine is also used for wheat breads, you may wish to consider buying a separate bread pan for gluten free baking.

MIXING THE INGREDIENTS FOR A BREAD MACHINE LOAF

- Stand the empty bread pan on weighing scales to measure the ingredients in your recipe.

- Omitting, swapping or not using the exact quantity of an ingredient can negatively affect the bake.

- Any dairy or plant milk can be used.

- Most types of vinegar can be used (malt vinegar may contain barley).

- All types of cooking oil can be used.

- Use whichever sized eggs you have available.

BAKING IN A BREAD MACHINE

- Select the gluten free setting on your machine if available. If not available, use the BASIC RAPID programme.

- Use the dark crust option on your bread machine for a golden loaf.

- After baking, rinse the machine pan in water only, avoid using detergent.

COOLING A BREAD MACHINE LOAF

- When the programme has finished, remove the bread pan from the machine immediately to avoid condensation and a soggy crust. Tip the bread out of the pan and remove the paddle before leaving it to cool.

- Leave gluten free bread to cool completely before slicing as the crumb structure continues to develop during cooling.

- For a softer crust, wrap hot bread in a clean tea towel and leave to cool.

Oven-baked Gluten Free Breads

Always select a bread recipe that uses gluten free flour rather than trying to adapt a recipe designed for wheat flour. Due to the batter used in most gluten free bread recipes it needs to be baked in a tin rather than as a free-form loaf.

MIXING THE INGREDIENTS

- Omitting an ingredient can affect the outcome of gluten free bread.

- Any dairy or plant milk can be used.

- Any type of vinegar can be used (malt vinegar may contain barley).

- Any type of cooking oil can be used.

- Mix your gluten free bread batter until smooth and lump free.

- Avoid adding extra flour to the batter to make a dough unless specified.

- Our recipes are tested using mixed size eggs, so use whichever size you have available.

KNEADING AND PROVING THE BATTER

- Most gluten free breads use a batter method which does not require kneading.

- Gluten free batters need a tin to hold the shape of the loaf.

- Proving times are given as a guide and the length of time will depend on the ambient temperature, which can cause the batter to rise more quickly or slowly than the time given in a recipe.

- When gluten free bread batter has risen to 7mm/¼ inch below the top of the tin, it is time to bake.

BAKING IN THE OVEN

- Preheat your oven 20 minutes before you want to bake.

- Our recipes are tested in bread tins measuring: 500g/1lb tin and 1kg/2lb tin.

COOLING AND STORING GLUTEN FREE BREAD

- Allow gluten free bread to cool completely on a wire rack before slicing.

- Gluten free bread is best eaten within 24 hours of baking.

- When the bread is cold, slice and open-freeze, then store in a polythene bag or wrapped in kitchen foil for up to 3 months. Unwrap and heat or toast frozen bread for 45–90 seconds.

USING LEFTOVER BREAD

- Cut off the bread crusts and, if the pieces are large enough, save them for toasting.

- Slice the bread and then cut the slices into chunks and use them as croutons.

- Using your fingers, break the chunks into crumbs or put the bread into a food processor and pulse to make gluten free breadcrumbs.

- Crusts, chunks and crumbs made from gluten free bread freeze well and are a useful ingredient that helps reduce waste. Bring them back to room temperature before using.

Pastry fundamentals & basic recipes

Shortcrust or sweet pastry, choux, flaky and hot-water raised pastry can all be made using gluten free flour, although these recipes and methods can differ from their conventional counterparts.

A chilled solid fat, such as butter, plant butter or lard, is best for gluten free pastry making, and be aware that the flours will absorb more liquid than wheat flour. Our top tips for success are:

- Avoid using any soft spread when making gluten free pastry as this can cause the pastry to become difficult to handle.

- Mix your pastry with a fork or pastry blender rather than your hands.

- A pinch of xanthan gum can help to bind gluten free pastry.

- Add enough water, a little more than conventional pastry, to make a slightly sticky dough, this will be absorbed by the flour during resting or chilling the pastry dough.

- Preheat your oven 20 minutes before you want to bake.

Pastry bakes can have a variety of textures, depending on how the pastry is made. **Shortcrust pastry** is typically used to bake an Apple Pie (page 171) or Quiche Lorraine (page 162), **flaky and puff pastry** to make Sausage Rolls (page 165), **choux pastry** in Chocolate Eclairs (page 182), **hot water pastry** for Raised Pork Pie (page 167), and **sweet pastry** for Mixed Berry Tart (page 203). Whatever type of gluten free pastry you make, here are the essentials.

MIXING THE PASTRY INGREDIENTS

- Chop the butter or plant butter into small cubes before adding it to the flour.

- Mix the flour and butter with a fork or pastry blender, rather than using your fingers, to avoid overmixing.

- Using a kitchen mixer can overwork gluten free pastry, making it hard when cooked.

- Gluten free pastry should be a little sticky before resting.

RESTING THE PASTRY

- Cover and rest gluten free pastry, according to the recipe, as the flour will absorb more liquid than pastry made with wheat flour.

ROLLING OUT THE PASTRY

- If the pastry is still slightly sticky after resting, dust the work surface and rolling pin with flour before rolling it out.

- Large pieces of gluten free pastry can be delicate to pick up but can be easily pressed into a pie dish or tart tin using your fingers.

- Pie tops can be rolled out between two pieces of baking liner or parchment.

CHILLING THE PASTRY DOUGH

- Flaky and puff pastry requires chilling before baking so the butter can react to the oven heat.

BAKING PASTRY

- Always preheat the oven to the temperature given in the recipe.

- Blind baking is a cooking technique used before the filling is added and helps to avoid a soggy base to the bake.

- If you don't have ceramic baking beans for blind baking, you can use rice, flour or the base of another baking tin instead.

STORING PASTRY

- Wrap unused pastry dough and store in the fridge for up to 24 hours.

- Raw pastry dough can be frozen for up to 3 months.

USING LEFTOVER PASTRY

- Pastry trimmings can be gathered up and re-rolled to make another tart or pie top decoration.

- Leftover pastry can also be rolled into a ball, wrapped and frozen for up to 3 months.

Shortcrust Pastry

OPTION:

200g FREEE Plain White Flour, plus extra
   for dusting
½ tsp FREEE Xanthan Gum
pinch of salt, optional
100g butter or plant butter, plus extra for tin
8–9 tbsp cold water

1   Preheat the oven to 180°C, Fan 160°C, 350°F, Gas 4 or according to your recipe. Rub a little butter around the inside of your baking dish or insert a baking liner.

2   Measure the flour, xanthan gum and salt, if making something savoury, into a bowl. Stir to combine and sift the flour blend into a mixing bowl.

3   Cut the butter into small cubes and add them to the bowl. Use a fork or pastry blender to work the butter into the flour until the mixture resembles breadcrumbs. Avoid using your fingers for this.

4   Stir in enough water to bring the pastry together into a soft, slightly sticky ball of dough – it will appear a little wet but will absorb liquid while resting. Cover the pastry dough and leave it to rest for 15 minutes.

5   Dust the work surface with flour, put the dough in the middle and sprinkle it with flour. Roll out the pastry into a circle 5cm/2 inches larger than your dish and lift it into the dish, or simply press it into the baking dish using your fingers.

6   Fill and bake according to your recipe.

Flaky Pastry

200g FREEE White Bread Flour,
  plus extra for dusting
pinch of salt
125g butter, chilled
1 egg
50ml water

1   Put the flour into a bowl, add the salt and stir to combine.

2   Cut the butter into very thin slices and lay these out on a plate. Add one-third of the slices to the bowl and, using a fork or pastry blender, work it into the flour until the mixture resembles fine breadcrumbs. Avoid using your fingers for this.

3   Break the egg into the bowl, add the water and stir to make a dough. Gather the mixture into a ball of soft dough. If the dough seems dry, add another teaspoon of water, or if it is excessively wet, cover and rest for 5 minutes.

4   Dust the work surface liberally with flour, place the dough in the middle and dust it with flour. Gently roll the dough into a 20 x 30cm /8 x 12 inch rectangle.

5   Lay half the remaining butter slices across the middle of the pastry, in lines just touching each other. Run a damp finger all around the outside of the pastry rectangle. Gently lift the left side of the pastry over and onto the middle of the butter. Now lift the right side of the pastry, folding it over so the butter is covered. Press around the edges and pinch any cracks to make sure no butter is exposed.

6   Gently fold the pastry in half, pinching any cracks to make sure no butter is exposed. Dust the pastry with flour, turn it over and dust the other side.

7   For the second time, roll the dough into a 20 x 30cm /8 x 12 inch rectangle. Arrange the remaining slices of butter in lines covering the middle of the pastry and finishing 1cm/ ⅜ inch from the sides. Run a damp finger all around the outside of the pastry rectangle. Carefully lift the left and right sides of the pastry over the butter to meet in the middle. Once again, press around the edges and pinch any cracks making sure no butter is exposed

8   Gently fold the pastry in half for a final time. Dust the folded pastry with flour, cover and chill for at least 10 minutes or up to 4 hours.

9   Use the pastry as per your recipe.

- -

Puff Pastry

200g FREEE White Bread Flour,
  plus extra for dusting
¼ tsp salt
150g butter, chilled
1 egg
50ml water

1   Put the flour into a bowl, add the salt and stir to combine.

2   Cut the butter into very thin slices and lay these out on a plate. Add one-third to the bowl and using a fork or pastry blender, work it into the flour until the mixture resembles fine breadcrumbs. Avoid using your fingers for this.

3   Break the egg into the bowl, add the water and stir to make a dough. If this does not happen easily add 1 teaspoon of water. If the dough seems dry, add another teaspoon of water, or if it is excessively wet, cover and rest for 5 minutes.

4   Dust the work surface liberally with flour, place the dough in the middle and dust the dough with flour. Gently roll the dough into a 20 x 30cm /8 x 12 inch rectangle.

5   Lay half the remaining butter slices across the middle of the pastry, in lines just touching each other. Run a damp finger all around the outside of the pastry rectangle. Gently lift the left side of the pastry over and onto the middle of the butter. Now lift the right side of the pastry, folding it over so the butter is covered. Press around the edges and pinch any cracks to make sure no butter is exposed.

6   Gently fold the pastry in half, pinching any cracks to make sure no butter is exposed. Dust the pastry with flour, turn it over and dust the other side.

7   For the second time, roll the dough into a 20 x 30cm /8 x 12 inch rectangle. Arrange the remaining slices of butter in lines covering the middle of the pastry and finishing 1cm/⅜ inch from the sides. Run a damp finger all around the outside of the pastry rectangle. Carefully lift the left and right sides of the pastry over the butter to meet in the middle. Once again, press around the edges and pinch any cracks making sure no butter is exposed.

8   Gently fold the pastry in half for a final time. Dust the folded pastry with flour and chill for at least 10 minutes or up to 4 hours.

- -

Sweet Pastry

100g FREEE Plain White Flour, plus extra
    for dusting
25g icing sugar
¼ tsp FREEE Xanthan Gum
50g butter, plus extra for tin
3 egg yolks

1   Preheat the oven to 190°C, Fan 170°C, 375°F, Gas 5 or according to your recipe. Rub a little butter around the inside of 20cm/ 8 inch round baking dish or tart tin or insert a baking liner.

2   Measure the flour, icing sugar and xanthan gum into a large bowl, stir to combine and sift into another bowl.

3   Cut the butter into small cubes and add them to the bowl. Using a fork or pastry blender, work them together until the mixture resembles fine breadcrumbs.

4   Add the egg yolks to the mixing bowl and stir to combine. Using your hands, gather everything together to form a smooth ball of pastry dough.

5   Dust the work surface with flour, put the dough in the middle and sprinkle it with flour. Roll out the pastry into a circle 5cm/2 inches larger than your dish and lift it into the dish, or simply press the pastry into the dish using your fingers. Cut away any pastry that hangs over the edge of the dish. Prick the pastry all over with a fork.

6   Blind bake or fill and bake according to your recipe.

- -

Choux Pastry

75g FREEE White Bread Flour
½ tsp caster sugar
2 eggs
50g butter
160ml water

1   Preheat the oven to 200°C, Fan 180°C, 400°F, Gas 6. Line a large baking tray with a baking liner or baking parchment.

2   Sift the flour into a bowl, sprinkle the sugar on top and put it beside the cooker.

3   Break the eggs into another bowl, beat them well and leave this bowl next to the cooker too.

4   Put the butter and water into a saucepan over a medium heat. When the butter has melted and the water has come to the boil, remove the pan from the heat. Immediately add the flour from the bowl and mix into a thick paste.

5   Return the pan to a gentle heat, stirring vigorously for 30 seconds, to make a soft dough. Remove the pan from the heat.

6   Add a third of the egg and beat it into the dough with a spatula. When it is incorporated, beat in another third of the egg. Beat in the remaining egg to make a thick, smooth paste.

7   Take a soup spoon of the paste, scrape it onto a second soup spoon, then scrape it back onto the original spoon to encourage the formation of a ball of choux paste.

8   Drop the ball of paste onto the baking tray and repeat with the remaining paste. Alternatively, put the choux paste into a piping bag and pipe balls of dough onto the baking tray.

9   Bake for 30–35 minutes until golden brown and crisp to the touch. Remove the tray from the oven.

10 As soon as you can handle the choux balls, cut the side of each bun with a sharp knife to allow the steam to escape.

11 Transfer the choux buns to a wire rack to cool.

12 When completely cool slice and fill the buns with a sweet or savoury filling.

Hot Water Pastry

300g FREEE White Bread Flour,
    plus extra for dusting
¼ tsp salt
125g lard
1 egg
200ml boiling water

1   Put the flour and salt into a bowl and stir to combine. Add the lard and use a fork or pastry blender to work it into the flour until the mixture resembles breadcrumbs. Avoid using your fingers for this.

2   Break the egg into a small bowl and beat to mix. Pour half the beaten egg into the mixing bowl and stir to roughly combine.

3   Add the boiling water and immediately stir to bring together a slightly sticky dough. Cover the dough and leave to stand for at least 1 hour.

4   Preheat the oven to 170°C, Fan 150°C, 325°F, Gas 3 or according to your recipe.

5   Press two-thirds of the pastry into a 15cm/ 6 inch round loose-bottomed tin. Tip the pie filling into the pastry lined tin and smooth the top. Brush the pastry rim with water.

6   Lightly dust a work surface with flour, put the remaining dough in the middle and sprinkle it with more flour. Roll the pastry into a 15cm /6 inch circle. Brush a little water around the circumference of the pastry circle. Press a 3cm /1¼ inch cookie cutter or egg cup into the centre of the pastry and remove the small pastry circle. This will allow steam to escape during cooking. Transfer the pastry circle over the filled pie, inverting it so the moistened side is down. Press, pinch or crimp together the outside edges using your fingers or the flat prongs of a fork.

7   Brush the remaining beaten egg over the top of the pie. Bake according to your recipe.

Sauce, gravy & batter fundamentals & basic recipes

Sauces and gravies hold together or are central to many sweet and savoury bakes, adding character and complementary flavours.

Sweet gluten free sauces are typically used inside bakes such as profiteroles, or on top of gluten free crumbles and other bakes. White or béchamel sauces and gravies can be made with gluten free flour blends, cornflour, rice flour, gram flour or xanthan gum, depending on dietary needs. Store leftover sauce, gravy or custard in the freezer for up to a month.

White Sauce using Gluten Free Plain Flour

OPTION:

A classic sauce for use on its own or with added cheese, parsley or mustard.

50g FREEE Plain White Flour
50g butter or plant butter
425ml milk or plant milk
salt and pepper

1   Put the flour, butter and milk into a saucepan over a medium heat, stirring all the time.

2   Continue stirring as the sauce thickens, bring to the boil and cook for a minute.

3   Remove the pan from the heat and season with salt and pepper to taste.

White Sauce using Cornflour

OPTION:

Simple and easy to make, you can also add sliced, cooked mushrooms or chopped anchovy.

500ml milk or plant milk
4 tbsp FREEE Cornflour
salt and pepper

1   Measure the milk into a saucepan, then remove 5 tablespoons of the milk to a heatproof bowl.

2   Heat the pan of milk until it is almost boiling, then take it off the heat.

3   Add the cornflour to the cold milk, stirring to make a smooth paste. Pour half of the hot milk onto the paste, stirring as you do this. Tip the mixture back into the saucepan.

4   Return the pan to the heat and stir as the sauce thickens. Allow the sauce to bubble gently and cook for a minute while stirring. Stir and season with salt and pepper.

Cheese Sauce using Xanthan Gum

This useful sauce is ideal for carbohydrate- and starch-free occasions.

25g butter
1 tsp FREEE Xanthan Gum
500ml milk
150g Cheddar, grated
salt and pepper
ground nutmeg, optional

1   Gently melt the butter, then leave in a heatproof bowl until cool but still runny.

2   Sift the xanthan gum over the butter and stir to make a smooth paste.

3   Measure half the milk into a saucepan.

4   Add the the remaining cold milk to the heatproof mixing bowl, a spoon at a time, beating vigorously with a whisk after each addition, to make a smooth paste.

5   Heat the saucepan of milk over a medium heat. When bubbles start to appear, pour a little milk into the mixing bowl and beat until smooth. Tip everything back into the saucepan, beating to combine. Bring to the boil and allow to cook gently for a minute. Remove from the heat and stir in the grated cheese.

6   Season with salt and pepper and a pinch of nutmeg if you like.

White Sauce using Rice Flour

OPTION: m

A neutral white sauce that can be flavored with miso, parsley or jam.

450ml milk or plant milk
4 tbsp FREEE Rice Flour
4 tbsp oil
salt and pepper, optional

1   Put the milk into a saucepan over a medium heat. When the milk is almost boiling, remove the pan from the heat.

2   Measure the rice flour and oil into a large bowl and mix to a smooth paste.

3   Pour half the warm milk onto the paste stirring as you do this. Tip the mixture back into the pan.

4   Return the pan to the heat and stir as the sauce thickens. Allow the sauce to bubble gently and cook for a minute while stirring. Season with salt and pepper to taste and serve.

Gram Flour Batter

Light and crispy, this batter is naturally egg and dairy free.

75g FREEE Gram Flour
½ tsp FREEE Bicarbonate of Soda
125ml water
oil, for frying

1   Measure the gram flour and bicarbonate of soda into a bowl, stir to combine and sift into a large mixing bowl.

2   Add half the water and stir to bring together a smooth and thick paste. Stir in the remaining water.

3   Put some oil in a frying pan over a medium heat.

4   Dip your item to be cooked in the batter, shake off any excess and slowly slide it into the hot pan. Cook over a medium heat, turning the item until golden on all sides, about 4–10 minutes depending on size and the temperature of the oil. Alternatively, you can cook battered items in a deep-fat fryer according to the manufacturer's instructions.

Gravy using Cornflour

Thicken cooking stock or roasting juices to make this easy sauce.

450ml gluten free stock
3 tsp FREEE Cornflour
3 tbsp cold water
salt and pepper
gluten free soy sauce, optional

1   Heat the stock in a saucepan.

2   Measure the cornflour and water into a small bowl and stir to make a smooth paste.

3   Stir about a cup of warm liquid into the cornflour paste. Immediately pour everything into the hot pan, stirring well. Return to the heat and bring to the boil while stirring as it cooks and thickens.

4   Season with salt and pepper and an optional splash of gluten free soy sauce.

Gravy using Xanthan Gum

For thickening stock or roasting juices on carbohydrate- and starch-free occasions.

1½ tbsp oil
1 tsp FREEE Xanthan Gum
250ml cold water or stock
250ml hot gluten free stock
salt and pepper
gluten free soy sauce or miso paste

1   Measure the oil into a large mixing bowl.

2   Sift the xanthan gum over the oil and stir to make a smooth paste.

3   Add the cold water to the mixing bowl, a spoon at a time, beating vigorously with a whisk after each addition, to make a smooth paste.

4   Heat the stock in a saucepan over a medium heat. When almost boiling, pour a little of the stock into the mixing bowl and beat until smooth. Pour everything back into the saucepan, beating to combine. Bring to the boil and allow to cook gently for a minute. Remove from the heat and season with salt and pepper.

5   Taste the gravy and season with gluten free soy sauce or miso.

Custard

OPTION: **m**

A popular accompaniment to puddings and baked desserts, but is also delicious cold.

450ml milk or plant milk
2 tbsp sugar
2 tsp vanilla extract
2-3 tbsp FREEE Cornflour

1   Measure the milk into a saucepan, then remove 5 tablespoons of the milk to a bowl. Add the sugar and vanilla extract to the saucepan.

2   Heat the pan of milk, stirring occasionally, until the sugar has dissolved. Bring the milk almost to the boil then take it off the heat.

3   Add the cornflour to the bowl of cold milk, stirring to make a smooth paste. Pour half of the warm milk onto the paste, stirring as you do this. Tip the mixture back into the saucepan.

4   Return the pan to the heat and stir as the custard thickens. Allow the custard to bubble gently and cook for a minute while stirring. Pour the custard into a jug and serve.

Creme Pâtissière

A thicker, richer custard mostly used inside or on top of cold, baked desserts.

25g icing sugar
2 tsp FREEE Cornflour
50ml cream
2 egg yolks
150ml milk
butter, for brushing

1   Measure the icing sugar, cornflour and cream into a large bowl, add the egg yolks and mix to a smooth paste.

2   Heat the milk in a saucepan until almost boiling. Pour half the hot milk onto the paste, stirring as you do this. Tip the mixture back into the saucepan.

3   Return the pan to a gentle heat and stir continuously as the custard thickens and cooks. Pour the custard into a clean bowl. To stop a skin forming, brush a little butter over a piece of baking parchment and put it, butter-side down, on the surface of the crème pâtissière to stop a skin forming. Leave until cool, then chill until required.

4   Before using, remove the parchment and beat the cold custard to ensure it is smooth.

CHAPTER 1

Cakes

Super delicious classic bakes
everyone will love. Layered cakes,
loaf cakes, muffins and showstopper
celebration cakes galore.

Victoria Sponge

This recipe uses the classic all-in-one method to make the sponge cake layers for a Victoria Sponge. The two sponges are traditionally sandwiched together with raspberry jam and cream, while the top is simply dusted with icing sugar.

SERVES: 8–12

Cake tin diameter	2 x 15cm (6 inch)	2 x 18cm (7 inch)	2 x 20cm (8 inch)
COOKING TIME (MINUTES)	25–30	30–35	35–40
butter, plus extra for tins	125g	175g	250g
FREEE Self Raising White Flour	125g	175g	250g
eggs	3	4	5
caster sugar	125g	175g	250g
FILLING:			
jam	3 tbsp	4 tbsp	5 tbsp
cream	25g	50g	75g
icing sugar	1 tsp	2 tsp	3 tsp

1 Preheat the oven to 180°C, Fan 160°C, 350°F, Gas 4. Select the tin size and ingredient quantity you plan to use and rub some butter around the inside of the tins.

2 Sift the flour into a large bowl.

3 Cut the butter into small cubes, put them into the mixing bowl and stir to cover them with flour.

4 Break the eggs into the bowl, add the sugar and beat everything together well.

5 Divide the mixture between the prepared baking tins and smooth the tops.

6 Bake for the time given for your chosen tin size until the cakes are just brown and start to come away from the sides of the tin. Turn the cakes out onto a wire rack, peel off the paper and leave to cool.

FILLING

7 Spread the jam onto one cool sponge.

8 Whip the cream and spread it over the jam. Place the second sponge on top.

9 Sift the icing sugar over the cake.

Coffee Cake

An easy-to-make cake with a deliciously tasty hint of coffee. Perfect for any get-together.

SERVES: 8–12
COOKING TIME: 20–25 MINUTES

2 tbsp coffee powder
2 tbsp boiling water
200g butter, plus extra for tins
200g caster sugar
4 eggs
200g FREEE Self Raising
   White Flour
250g full-fat cream cheese
1 tsp icing sugar

1   Preheat the oven to 190°C, Fan 170°C, 375°F, Gas 5. Rub some butter around the inside of two 20cm/8 inch round baking tins or insert a baking liner.

2   Put the coffee into a cup, add the boiling water, stir to make a paste and leave to cool.

3   Cut the butter into small cubes and put them into a mixing bowl. Add the caster sugar and beat with an electric whisk until light and fluffy.

4   Beat in the eggs one at a time.

5   Sift the flour into the bowl and beat again.

6   Add the coffee mixture and stir until everything is well combined.

7   Divide the mixture between the prepared tins and smooth the top.

8   Bake for 20–25 minutes. If a cocktail stick pressed into the centre of the cake comes out clean, it is ready. Leave the sponges to cool a little in the tins before turning them onto a wire rack to cool completely.

9   Spread the cream cheese on one cool sponge layer and place the second sponge layer on top. Sift the icing sugar over the top of the cake.

Black Forest Gateau

A classic combination of black cherries, cream and chocolate, this cake makes a lovely showstopper bake for a party or special occasion.

SERVES: 8–12
COOKING TIME: 70–75 MINUTES

400g tin black cherries
250g butter, plus extra for tins
175g FREEE Self Raising
   White Flour
½ tsp FREEE Baking Powder
5 eggs
250g caster sugar
50g cocoa powder
3 tbsp milk
3 tbsp kirsch

CHERRY CREAM:
100g icing sugar
300ml double cream

DECORATION:
50g dark chocolate
150g fresh black cherries

1   Drain the cherry juice into a jug. Stone and finely chop the cherries into a sieve standing over a bowl. Leave the juice to drain for the cherry filling.

2   Chop the butter into cubes and allow it to come to room temperature. Preheat the oven to 180°C, Fan 160°C, 350°F, Gas 4. Rub some butter around the base and sides of a 20cm/8 inch deep, round baking tin or insert a baking liner.

3   Measure the flour and baking powder into a bowl, stir to combine, then sift into another bowl.

4   Separate the eggs, putting the whites in one mixing bowl and the yolks into another.

5   Tip the chopped butter cubes onto the yolks, add the caster sugar and beat together until smooth. Pour 125ml of the drained cherry juice into the bowl and beat until combined.

6   Sift the cocoa into the bowl and beat again until smooth.

7   Tip the flour mixture into the bowl and beat everything together well. Stir in the milk.

8   Clean the beaters, then beat the egg whites until stiff. Using a metal spoon, take a quarter of the egg white and fold it roughly into the mixing bowl with a cutting and turning action. Repeat with a second quarter of egg white, then add the remaining egg white, cutting and folding everything together without knocking out the air.

9   Tip the mixture into the prepared tin and smooth the top.

10 Bake for 70–75 minutes or until the cake starts to come away from the sides of the tin and a cocktail stick, inserted into the centre comes out clean. Leave to cool in the tin.

Continued overleaf →

----

11 When cool, turn the cake out of the tin, peel off any paper and slice it horizontally into 3 discs of sponge. Measure the kirsch into a cup, then paint it over the sponges using a pastry brush.

FOR THE CHERRY CREAM:

12 Press the draining chopped cherries to expel any remaining liquid then tip them into a bowl.

13 Measure the icing sugar into another bowl. Add half of the sugar to the cherries.

14 Whip the cream until thick, then beat in the remaining icing sugar into the cream. Tip the cherry mixture into the cream and stir to combine.

FOR THE FILLING AND DECORATION:

15 Break the chocolate into cubes. Put the chocolate pieces into a small heatproof bowl and microwave on full power until the chocolate is soft, about 60–70 seconds. Pour the chocolate onto the back of a baking tray or a piece of baking parchment. Spread the chocolate out thinly and leave to chill.

16 When cold and set, break the chocolate into shards.

17 Spoon a third of the cherry cream onto the kirsch-soaked sponges, spreading it out to the edges with a palette knife. Carefully lift one on top of the other, add the final sponge, then press gently so that a little cream squidges out of each layer.

18 Pile the remaining cherry cream on top, spreading it out and just over the edges of the sponge. Using a palette knife, run it around the outside edges of the cake, smearing some cherry cream all around the outside.

19 Press chocolate shards into the outside edge of the cake. Decorate with fresh cherries on top to serve.

Banana Bundt Cake with Toffee Icing

Using a shaped silicone or metal Bundt tin adds some wow factor to the ever-popular banana bread. A fun way to enjoy an everyday treat as well as an ideal bake for a special occasion.

SERVES: 8–12
COOKING TIME:
50–55 MINUTES FOR METAL TIN OR 45–50 MINUTES FOR SILICONE MOULD

oil, for tin
2 ripe bananas
100g butter
100g soft brown sugar
1 tsp vanilla extract
2 eggs
200g FREEE Self Raising White Flour

ICING:
75g butter
75g brown sugar
50g double cream

1   Preheat the oven to 180°C, Fan 160°C, 350°F, Gas 4. Rub some oil around the inside of a 20cm/8 inch metal Bundt tin or silicone mould.

2   Peel and mash the bananas on a plate.

3   Chop the butter into cubes and put them into a mixing bowl. Add the sugar and beat together until smooth.

4   Add the mashed banana and vanilla and beat again.

5   Break the eggs into the bowl, one at a time, ensuring each is well incorporated before adding the next.

6   Sift the flour into the bowl and stir the mixture.

7   Tip the mixture into the prepared Bundt tin or silicone mould and smooth the top.

8   Bake in the metal Bundt tin for 50-55 minutes or in the silicone mould for 45-50 minutes, or until the sponge springs back when touched. Leave the cake to cool in the tin (or mould) for 40 minutes, then carefully turn it out onto a wire rack to cool completely.

FOR THE ICING:

9   Chop the butter into cubes and put them into a saucepan. Add the sugar and cream. Put the pan over a gentle heat and stir to make a smooth sauce. Remove the pan from the heat. Stir as the icing cools and thickens slightly.

10 Gently pour the icing over the top of the cool Bundt cake, allowing it to run down the sides. Leave the icing to set, then store in a tin until ready to serve.

Apple and Blackberry Cake

A classic combination that heralds the autumn, a slice of this apple and blackberry cake is delicious with a hot drink or could be served drizzled with a little cream or custard (see page 31).

SERVES: 8–12
COOKING TIME: 65–70 MINUTES

225g FREEE Self Raising
   White Flour
1 tbsp ground cinnamon
½ tsp FREEE Xanthan Gum
2 apples
3 eggs
150g caster sugar
100ml oil, plus extra for tin
100g blackberries

BLACKBERRY TOPPING:
100g blackberries
125g icing sugar
½ tsp finely grated lemon rind

1   Preheat the oven to 190°C, Fan 170°C, 375°F, Gas 5. Rub some oil around the inside of a 20cm/8 inch deep round cake tin or insert a baking liner.

2   Measure the flour, cinnamon and xanthan gum into a bowl, blend together well and sift into another bowl.

3   Peel, core and chop the apples into small cubes, then stir the cubes into the flour.

4   Break the eggs into another mixing bowl, add the sugar and oil and beat together.

5   Tip the prepared flour and apples into the bowl and stir to combine.

6   Add the blackberries and stir gently. Transfer the mixture to the prepared tin and smooth the top.

7   Bake for 65–70 minutes until a cocktail stick inserted into the centre comes out clean. Leave to cool in the tin, then turn out onto a wire rack to cool completely.

FOR THE TOPPING:
8   Divide the blackberries in half.

9   Put the icing sugar into a bowl, add the lemon rind and half of the berries. Mash together to form an icing, then spread it over the top of the cold cake.

10 Press the remaining blackberries into the icing to decorate.

Sticky Toffee Layer Cake

This spectacular three-layer cake makes the perfect birthday treat, especially for lovers of the classic sticky toffee pudding!

OPTION:

SERVES: 10–12
COOKING TIME: 35–40 MINUTES

oil, for tins
225g stoned dates
1 tsp FREEE Bicarbonate of
    Soda
250ml boiling water
225g butter or plant butter
200g soft brown sugar
3 eggs (or 3 tbsp FREEE Gram
    Flour mixed with 6 tbsp water)
225g FREEE Self Raising
    White Flour
3 tbsp black treacle

WHITE CHOCOLATE FILLING:
500g mascarpone (or 400g
    plant cream cheese plus
    100g plant cream)
200g white chocolate
    (or 100g cashew nut butter
    plus 100g icing sugar plus
    2 tsp vanilla extract)

TOFFEE TOPPING:
150g brown sugar
100g cream or plant cream
100g butter or plant butter

As with many of our recipes, use our ingredient swaps to make this cake vegan.

1 Preheat the oven to 180°C, Fan 160°C, 350°F, Gas 4. Rub some oil around the inside of three 20cm/8 inch round, loose-bottomed cake tins or insert a baking liner.

2 Chop the dates into a bowl, add the bicarbonate of soda and stir in the boiling water. Leave to cool, then blend into a purée.

3 Cut the butter into small cubes and put them into a mixing bowl. Add the sugar and beat together well.

4 Break the eggs into the bowl, one at a time, beating well after each addition (or add the gram flour and water and beat well).

5 Beat in half the flour, then the black treacle followed by the remaining flour. Add the cold date purée and mix well.

6 Divide the mixture between the three prepared tins and smooth the tops. Bake for 35–40 minutes. Turn the cakes out onto a wire rack to cool.

FOR THE WHITE CHOCOLATE FILLING:
7 Put the mascarpone into a bowl and loosen it with a fork.

8 Break the white chocolate into another heatproof bowl and microwave for 40–50 seconds. Stir gently to ensure all is melted. Stir the chocolate into the mascarpone.

9 Divide the mixture between the three cool sponges, smoothing it out to the edges. Pile the cake layers on top of each other. Chill the cake in the freezer for 30 minutes.

FOR THE TOFFEE TOPPING:
10 Put the sugar, cream and butter into a saucepan, bring to a vigorous foaming boil and cook for 90 seconds, stirring constantly. Remove the pan from the heat and stir until the topping cools and thickens.

11 Spoon the syrup over the top of the cake, allowing a little to dribble down the sides.

White Chocolate Layer Cake

A showstopper bake for white chocolate lovers, with three layers of sponge this cake is ideal for a celebration or special teatime treat which everyone can enjoy. Serve with a cup of tea or coffee or, for a lovely summer dessert, serve slices of white chocolate cake with a few raspberries and a jug of cream.

SERVES: 8–12
COOKING TIME: 20–25 MINUTES

175g FREEE Self Raising
   White Flour
175g butter, plus extra for tins
3 eggs
175g caster sugar
1 tbsp vanilla extract
3 tbsp milk

WHITE CHOCOLATE BUTTERCREAM:
50g butter
50g icing sugar
2 tsp milk
50g white chocolate

WHITE ICING:
75g butter
75g icing sugar
100g full-fat cream cheese

WHITE CHOCOLATE DRIP AND
DECORATIVE SHARDS:
90g white chocolate
50ml double cream

1   Preheat the oven to 180°C, Fan 160°C, 350°F, Gas 4. Rub some butter around the inside of three 18cm/7 inch round cake tins or insert a baking liner.

2   Sift the flour into a large bowl.

3   Cut the butter into small cubes, put them into the mixing bowl and stir to cover them with flour.

4   Break the eggs into the bowl, add the sugar and vanilla and beat everything together until smooth.

5   Add the milk and mix well.

6   Divide the mixture between the prepared baking tins and smooth the top.

7   Bake for 20–25 minutes until the cakes are just brown and start to come away from the sides of the tins. Turn the cakes out onto a wire rack, peel off the liner and leave to cool.

FOR THE BUTTERCREAM:

8   Cut the butter into small cubes, then put them in a mixing bowl. Add the icing sugar and milk and beat until smooth.

9   Coarsely grate the white chocolate into the mixing bowl and mix together well.

10 Divide the white chocolate buttercream filling between the top of the cool sponges, spreading it out over each one. Place the sponges one on top of the other and leave to set.

Continued overleaf →

White Chocolate Layer Cake continued

FOR THE WHITE ICING:

11 Chop the butter into cubes and put them into a mixing bowl. Beat the butter until it is smooth. Add the icing sugar and beat until combined.

12 Measure the cream cheese into the bowl and beat everything until smooth.

13 Gently spread half of the white icing around the sides of the cake. Spread the remaining icing over the top of the cake.

FOR THE WHITE CHOCOLATE DRIP AND DECORATIVE SHARDS:

14 Break the white chocolate into cubes, put 15g in one bowl and 75g in another.

15 Microwave the bowl of 15g on full power until the chocolate is soft, about 60–80 seconds. Pour the chocolate onto a marble tile, the back of a baking tray or a piece of baking parchment. Spread the chocolate out thinly. Leave to cool. When cold, break the chocolate into triangular shards.

16 Put the cream into a saucepan over a medium heat. When the cream comes to the boil, remove the pan from the heat. Immediately tip the 75g bowl of chocolate cubes into the hot cream, shake the pan and leave for 5 minutes. Gently stir the cream and chocolate until smooth.

17 Leave to cool and thicken then pour around the circumference of the cake, allowing it to drip down the sides.

18 Gently press the white chocolate shards into the top of the cake around the circumference.

Chocolate Cake

An absolutely gorgeous chocolate cake with three lovely sponge layers – you would never know it's gluten free.

SERVES: 8–12
COOKING TIME: 35–40 MINUTES

75g cocoa powder
250g FREEE Self Raising
    White Flour
325g caster sugar
4 eggs
200ml milk
200ml oil, plus extra for tins
1 tbsp vanilla extract
125ml boiling water

FILLING AND TOPPING:
250g dark cooking chocolate
250ml double cream
100g caster sugar

1   Preheat the oven to 180°C, Fan 160°C, 350°F, Gas 4. Rub some oil around the inside of three 20cm/8 inch round cake tins or insert baking liners.

2   Measure the cocoa and flour into a bowl, stir to combine, then sift into another mixing bowl.

3   Add the caster sugar and stir with a whisk to combine.

4   Break the eggs into a large jug, add the milk, oil and vanilla and beat together well.

5   Pour the egg mixture into the mixing bowl and mix everything together with the whisk.

6   Add the boiling water and beat well.

7   Divide the runny mixture between the tins.

8   Bake for 35–40 minutes. Leave the cakes in their tins to cool for a couple of minutes, then turn them out onto a wire rack to cool completely.

FOR THE FILLING AND TOPPING:
9   Break the chocolate into squares.

10 Put the cream and sugar into a saucepan and stir over a medium heat until about to boil. Remove the pan from the heat, add the chocolate and stir until combined. Leave to cool, stirring regularly until a thick paste starts to form, this may take 8–10 minutes.

11 Put a quarter of the icing onto the top of each cold sponge and spread it out to the edges. Place the sponges on top of each other, spread the last quarter of icing around the outside of the cake and transfer it to a cake stand. Working quickly, gently press the back of a small teaspoon into the middle of the cake as you turn the stand, to create a circular pattern in the icing.

Images overleaf →

Lemon Drizzle Loaf Cake

A true classic! Perfect with a cup of tea and you will never know this is gluten free.

SERVES: 8–12
COOKING TIME: 45–50 MINUTES

175g FREEE Plain White Flour
½ tsp FREEE Bicarbonate of
    Soda
150g butter, plus extra for tin
150g caster sugar
3 eggs
2 lemons

DRIZZLE:
75ml lemon juice
75g caster sugar

ICING:
1 lemon
75g icing sugar

1. Preheat the oven to 180°C, Fan 160°C, 350°F, Gas 4. Rub some butter around the inside of a 900g/2lb loaf tin or insert a baking liner.

2. Measure the flour and bicarbonate of soda into a bowl and stir to combine.

3. Put the butter and sugar into another mixing bowl and beat together until light and fluffy.

4. Beat in the eggs one at a time, ensuring each is well incorporated before adding the next.

5. Sift the prepared flour into the mixing bowl and stir to combine.

6. Finely grate the lemon rind and squeeze the juice. Save the juice for later. Add the rind and any lemon pulp to the mixing bowl and mix well.

7. Tip the mixture into the prepared loaf tin and smooth the top.

8. Bake for 45–50 minutes until a cocktail stick pressed into the sponge comes out clean. Leave the cake to cool in the tin.

FOR THE DRIZZLE:

9. Pour the reserved lemon juice into a jug and, if necessary, add more lemon juice to make it up to 75ml.

10. Measure the sugar into a saucepan, add the lemon juice and cook over a medium heat. Shake the pan occasionally and when the sugar is dissolved, boil for a minute to make a syrup.

11. Prick all over the surface of the cake with a cocktail stick, pressing right through the cake. Pour the syrup slowly all over the top of the cake and leave to cool in the tin.

FOR THE ICING:

12. Cut thin slices of rind from the lemon and squeeze the juice. Put the icing sugar in a bowl, add 3–4 teaspoons of lemon juice and stir to a thick consistency that flows slightly. Spread the icing over the top of the cake, allowing it to dribble down the sides. Scatter the lemon rind over. Leave to set before serving.

Madeira Loaf Cake

The creamy light texture of this Madeira sponge makes a sensational loaf cake that keeps extremely well. We think this classic sponge is best served in simple slices.

g

SERVES: 8–12
COOKING TIME: 65–70 MINUTES

150g butter, plus extra for tin
150g caster sugar
3 eggs
finely grated rind of ½ lemon
15g ground almonds
100g FREEE Self Raising
   White Flour
2 tbsp milk

1   Preheat the oven to 170°C, Fan 150°C, 325°F, Gas 3. Rub some butter around the inside of a 450g/1lb loaf tin or insert a baking liner.

2   Cut the butter into small cubes and put them into a mixing bowl. Add the caster sugar and beat together until light and fluffy.

3   Break one egg into the bowl and beat well.

4   Put the lemon rind into the bowl, add the ground almonds and stir to combine.

5   Beat in the remaining eggs one at a time.

6   Sift the flour into the bowl and mix well.

7   Stir in the milk.

8   Tip the mixture into the prepared baking tin and smooth the top.

9   Bake for 65–70 minutes until a cocktail stick pushed into the centre comes out clean. Leave to cool in the tin for 10 minutes before turning out onto a wire rack to cool completely.

Earl Grey Fruit Loaf

A delicious fruit loaf infused with Earl Grey tea that combines delicate citrus, bergamot notes with the woody flavour of tea. Serve the tea loaf in simple slices or spread lightly with butter, to accompany a cup of your favourite tea.

OPTION:

SERVES: 8–12
COOKING TIME: 70–75 MINUTES

2 Earl Grey teabags
200ml boiling water
4 tbsp oil, plus extra for tin
300g mixed dried fruits:
    sultanas, raisins, prunes,
    dates and apricots
200g FREEE Plain White Flour
2 tsp FREEE Baking Powder
100g soft brown sugar
finely grated rind and juice of
    ½ orange
1 egg (or 1 tbsp FREEE Gram
    Flour mixed with 2 tbsp
    water)

1. Put the teabags into a jug, add the boiling water and leave to stand for 10 minutes.

2. Preheat the oven to 180°C, Fan 160°C, 350°F, Gas 4. Rub some oil around the inside of a 900g/2lb loaf tin or insert a baking liner.

3. Weigh the dried fruits into a bowl. If using prunes, dates or apricots, cut these into quarters. Pour the tea into the bowl and leave until completely cool.

4. Sift the flour and baking powder into another bowl, add the sugar and mix together.

5. Add the orange rind and juice to the bowl. Add the egg (or gram flour and water) and oil and beat well.

6. Discard the teabags and stir the soaked fruit and liquid into the bowl.

7. Tip the mixture into the prepared tin and smooth the top.

8. Bake for 70–75 minutes. Leave the cake to cool in the tin for 10 minutes, then gently turn it out onto a wire rack to cool completely.

Banana and Chocolate Chip Loaf Cake

A delicious loaf cake made using our FREEE Self Raising Flour. As an alternative to the coconut oil used in the recipe, butter or a plant butter can also be used. Perfect as a weekend treat!

SERVES: 8–12
COOKING TIME: 50–55 MINUTES

2 ripe bananas
100g coconut oil, plus extra for tin
100g caster sugar
2 eggs
200g FREEE Self Raising White Flour
100g milk or dark chocolate chips
1 tsp icing sugar

1   Preheat the oven to 180°C, Fan 160°C, 350°F, Gas 4. Rub some oil around the inside of a 900g/2lb loaf tin or insert a baking liner.

2   Peel and mash the bananas.

3   Put the oil and sugar into a mixing bowl and beat together. Add the mashed bananas and beat again.

4   Break the eggs into the bowl, one at a time, ensuring each is well incorporated before adding the next.

5   Sift the flour into the bowl and stir the mixture.

6   Stir in the chocolate chips.

7   Tip the mixture into the prepared tin and smooth the top.

8   Bake for 50-55 minutes until the sponge springs back when touched. Leave to cool in the tin for 1 hour, then transfer to a wire rack to cool completely.

9   Sift the icing sugar over the top of the cake to serve.

Carrot Loaf Cake

Carrots, raisins and pecan nuts combine in this popular cut-and-come-again loaf cake.

SERVES: 8–12
COOKING TIME: 60–65 MINUTES

100g FREEE Self Raising
   White Flour
100g soft brown sugar
1 tsp ground cinnamon
25g pecans
25g raisins
150g carrots
2 eggs
75ml oil, plus extra for tin
1 tsp vanilla extract

CREAM CHEESE TOPPING:
100g icing sugar
125g full-fat cream cheese
25g pecans

1   Preheat the oven to 180°C, Fan 160°C, 350°F, Gas 4. Rub some oil around the inside of a 450g/1lb loaf tin or insert a baking liner.

2   Measure the flour, sugar and cinnamon into a bowl, stir to combine and sift into another mixing bowl.

3   Finely grate the carrots into another bowl. Break the eggs into the bowl, add the oil and vanilla and beat together well.

4   Dice the pecans and add these to the bowl with the raisins.

5   Add the prepared flour blend and mix to combine.

6   Tip the mixture into the prepared loaf tin and smooth the top.

7   Bake for 60–65 minutes. Leave to cool in the tin.

FOR THE TOPPING:

8   Sift the icing sugar into a bowl. Add the cream cheese and stir until combined. Spread the topping over the top of the cool cake. Or beat the cream cheese and icing sugar together until light and fluffy. Scoop everything into a piping bag with a 7mm/¼ inch nozzle and pipe in a zig zag over the top of the cool cake.

9   Finely dice the pecans and sprinkle them over the top.

Double Chocolate Cupcake Muffins

Ten wonderful cupcake muffins, made with gluten free flour, which will please any chocolate lover. We like to use dark chocolate chips inside and white chocolate chips on top, although you can use any kind you fancy!

MAKES: 10
COOKING TIME: 20–22 MINUTES

75g FREEE Plain White Flour
2 tbsp cocoa powder
2 tsp FREEE Baking Powder
100g sugar
50g chocolate chips
2 eggs
4 tbsp oil
1 tbsp water
1 tsp vanilla extract
25g white chocolate chips for topping

1 Preheat the oven to 190°C, Fan 170°C, 375°F, Gas 5. Stand 10 cupcake cases in the holes of a muffin or tart tray.

2 Measure the flour, cocoa and baking powders into a bowl, stir to combine and sift into a mixing bowl. Add the sugar and chocolate chips and stir again.

3 Break the eggs into another bowl. Add the oil, water and vanilla extract and beat together really well.

4 Tip onto the prepared flour blend and mix well.

5 Divide the mixture between the prepared muffin cases. Scatter the white chocolate chips over the top of each cupcake.

6 Bake for 20–22 minutes.

Carrot Cake Muffins

These carrot cupcake muffins are a great snack to enjoy with a cup of coffee or your favourite tea. They are also pretty good for breakfast on the run or as a lunchbox treat.

MAKES: 6
COOKING TIME: 25–35 MINUTES

150g FREEE Plain White Flour
100g brown sugar
1 tbsp FREEE Baking Powder
1 tsp ground cinnamon
100g carrots
1 egg
50ml oil
1 tbsp finely grated orange rind
4 tbsp orange juice

CREAM CHEESE TOPPING:
25g icing sugar
100g full-fat cream cheese

1 Preheat the oven to 190°C, Fan 170°C, 375°F, Gas 5. Stand 6 cupcake cases in the holes of a muffin or tart tray.

2 Measure the flour, sugar, baking powder and cinnamon into a bowl and stir to combine.

3 Finely grate the carrots into a mixing bowl or blender and break the egg into the bowl.

4 Add the oil, half the orange rind and all the orange juice and beat together well.

5 Add the prepared flour blend and mix again.

6 Divide the mixture between the cupcake cases.

7 Bake for 25–35 minutes.

FOR THE CREAM CHEESE TOPPING:

8 Sift the icing sugar into a bowl. Add the cream cheese and stir until combined. Spread the topping over the cold cupcakes.

9 Sprinkle the remaining orange rind over the top.

Blueberry Muffins

The fresh blueberries added to these muffins become juicy, fruity mouthfuls nestling in the sweet, soft muffin sponge.

MAKES: 6
COOKING TIME: 20–25 MINUTES

50ml oil
2 tbsp natural yoghurt
100g caster sugar
1 egg
150g FREEE Self Raising
    White Flour
100g fresh blueberries
icing sugar, for dusting

1   Preheat the oven to 190°C, Fan 170°C, 375°F, Gas 5. Stand 6 paper muffin cases in the holes of a muffin or tart tray.

2   Put the oil, yoghurt, sugar and egg into a large bowl and beat together well.

3   Add the flour and stir to combine. Stir in the blueberries.

4   Divide the mixture between the prepared muffin cases.

5   Bake for 20–25 minutes.

6   Sift a little icing sugar over the cool muffins before serving.

Simnel Cake

Here is a gluten free version of this traditional Easter celebration cake. Simnel cakes are a spicy fruit cake with a marzipan layer baked into the middle. The 11 marzipan balls that decorate the top are said to represent the true disciples.

OPTION:

SERVES: 8–12
COOKING TIME: 1½–1¾ HOURS

400g marzipan, or egg free
    marzipan
icing sugar, for dusting
175g FREEE Self Raising
    White Flour
1 tsp FREEE Xanthan Gum
1 tsp mixed spice
1 apple
150g caster sugar
125ml oil, plus extra for tin
75ml water
300g mixed dried fruit

TOPPING:
2 tsp apricot jam

1 Preheat the oven to 170°C, Fan 150°C, 325°F, Gas 3. Rub some oil around the inside of a 20cm/8 inch round deep cake tin or insert a baking liner.

2 Take 100g of the marzipan and divide it into 11 small pieces. Roll the small pieces into small balls.

3 Dust the work surface with a little icing sugar, take half of the remaining marzipan and roll into a circle just larger than the cake tin. Place the tin on top of the marzipan circle and cut around the outside to make a perfect circle. Cover and set aside all the marzipan.

4 Put the flour, xanthan gum and mixed spice into a bowl and stir to combine.

5 Peel and grate the apple into a large mixing bowl, add the sugar, oil and water and beat well.

6 Add the prepared flour to the bowl and beat well.

7 Stir in the mixed dried fruit. Tip half the mixture into the prepared cake tin and smooth the top.

8 Take the prepared marzipan circle and place it on the cake mixture.

9 Put the remaining cake mixture onto the marzipan and smooth the surface.

10 Bake for 1½–1¾ hours. Leave to cool in the tin for at least 30 minutes, then turn out onto a wire rack to cool completely.

FOR THE TOPPING:
11 Warm the apricot jam and brush half over the top of the cool cake.

12 Roll the remaining marzipan into a circle just larger than the cake tin. Place the tin on top and cut a zigzag pattern around the outside. Gently lift the marzipan on top of the cake.

13 Brush the base of each prepared marzipan ball with jam and place them in a circle on the top of the cake.

14 Place the cake under a hot grill for a few minutes to lightly brown the marzipan.

15 Store the cool cake in an airtight tin.

Cocoa and Vanilla Swiss Roll

This classic cake can make a special occasion of morning coffee or afternoon tea. A Cocoa and Vanilla Swiss Roll cake is the ideal celebration treat and is also the basis for the traditional Chocolate Yule Log on page 76.

SERVES: 8–12
COOKING TIME: 13–15 MINUTES

butter, for baking tray
25g cocoa powder
5 tbsp boiling water
5 eggs
125g caster sugar
125g FREEE Self Raising
    White Flour

VANILLA BUTTERCREAM FILLING:
175g icing sugar, plus 1 tbsp for
    dusting
125g butter, softened
1 tsp vanilla extract

1 Preheat the oven to 200°C, Fan 180°C, 400°F, Gas 6. Rub some butter around the inside of a 23 x 33cm/9 x 13 inch baking tray or Swiss roll tin, or insert a baking liner.

2 Put the cocoa and boiling water into a bowl, mix into a smooth paste and set aside.

3 Break the eggs into a large bowl and whisk using an electric whisk. Add the caster sugar and whisk for a minute.

4 Sift the flour into the bowl and whisk lightly.

5 Add the prepared cocoa mixture and whisk again.

6 Tip the mixture into the prepared tray and spread it out to the edges.

7 Bake for 13–15 minutes. Leave the cake to cool in the tray for 2–3 minutes.

8 Spread a clean tea towel over the baking tray, place a chopping board on top and invert everything together. Remove the baking tray, and baking liner, if used, to leave the sponge on the tea towel. Using the tea towel for support, roll from the short end of the sponge to make a cylinder with the cloth inside. Leave the cloth and sponge cylinder to cool completely.

FOR THE VANILLA BUTTERCREAM FILLING:

9 Sift the icing sugar into a mixing bowl, add the softened butter and vanilla. Beat together until smooth.

10 Gently unroll the cool sponge, spread the buttercream evenly over the inside, then roll the sponge up quite tightly from the short end, making sure the filling stays inside. You can use the tea towel to help with this.

11 Sift icing sugar over the Swiss roll to serve.

Chocolate Yule Log

Nothing says Christmas like a Chocolate Yule Log – simply delicious and you'll never know this is gluten free. This cake can be served with a simple dusting of icing sugar.

SERVES: 8–12
COOKING TIME: 13–15 MINUTES

butter, for baking tray
35g cocoa powder
5 tbsp boiling water
5 eggs
125g caster sugar
125g FREEE Self Raising
   White Flour

VANILLA BUTTERCREAM FILLING:
175g icing sugar
125g butter, softened
1 tsp vanilla extract

YULE LOG TOPPING:
100ml double cream
200g milk chocolate
crystalised fruits or herbs
   (see page 79, optional)
1 tbsp icing sugar

1 Preheat the oven to 200°C, Fan 180°C, 400°F, Gas 6. Rub some butter around the inside of a 23 x 33cm/9 x 13 inch baking tray or insert a baking liner.

2 Put the cocoa and boiling water into a bowl, mix until smooth, then set aside.

3 Break the eggs into a large bowl and beat really well.

4 Add the caster sugar and beat for 2 minutes.

5 Sift the flour into the bowl and beat for another 2 minutes. Add the prepared cocoa mixture and beat for a further minute.

6 Tip the mixture into the prepared tray and spread it out to the edges.

7 Bake for 13–15 minutes. Leave the cake in the tray to cool for 2 minutes.

8 Spread a clean tea towel over the baking tray, place a chopping board on top and invert everything together. Remove the baking tray, and baking liner if used, to leave the sponge on the tea towel. Using the tea towel for support, roll from the short end of the sponge to make a cylinder with the cloth inside. Leave the cloth and sponge cylinder to cool completely.

FOR THE VANILLA BUTTERCREAM FILLING:
9 Sift the icing sugar into a bowl, add the softened butter and vanilla. Beat together until smooth.

10 Gently unroll the cool sponge, spread the buttercream evenly over the top, then roll the sponge up quite tightly from the short end, making sure the filling stays inside. You can use the tea towel to help with this.

FOR THE YULE LOG TOPPING:

11 Put the cream into a saucepan, bring it to the boil, then remove it from the heat and add the chocolate. Stir until smooth. Cool the mixture for a few minutes, stirring occasionally as it thickens.

12 Spread the topping over the cake. Drag the prongs of a fork lengthways through the topping to create a log-like texture.

13 If adding frosted fruits or herbs, press them into the topping. Chill until set.

14 Sift a light dusting of icing sugar over the cake to serve.

Christmas Cake

Packed with mixed dried fruits, this is a typical cake for Christmas and other important celebrations. This cake is decorated with crystalised cranberries and rosemary fronds.

SERVES: 10–14
COOKING TIME: 2–2¼ HOURS

100g glacé cherries, halved
500g mixed dried fruit
100g flaked or ground almonds
finely grated rind and juice of
    1 lemon
2 tbsp brandy or apple juice
150g FREEE Plain White Flour
1 tsp mixed spice
125g butter
125g soft brown sugar
3 eggs

ICING:
3 tbsp apricot jam
icing sugar, for dusting
400g marzipan
500g fondant icing

CRYSTALISED CRANBERRY AND
ROSEMARY DECORATION:
25g caster sugar, plus extra for
    dusting
100g granulated sugar
2 tbsp water
fresh rosemary fronds
fresh cranberries

1   Preheat the oven to 150°C, Fan 130°C, 300°F, Gas 2. Line the base and sides of a 20cm/8 inch deep, round cake tin with a double layer of baking parchment or greaseproof paper.

2   Cut a 30cm/12 inch square of parchment, greaseproof or brown paper, fold the corners to meet in the middle, press to make folded flaps and save for later.

3   Measure the halved cherries, mixed dried fruit and almonds into the bowl. Add the lemon rind and juice to the bowl, add the brandy or fruit juice and stir to combine.

4   Measure the flour and mixed spice into another bowl, stir to mix and set aside.

5   Put the butter and sugar into a large mixing bowl and beat together until light and fluffy.

6   Beat in the eggs one at a time, ensuring each is well incorporated before adding the next.

7   Add the prepared flour and beat again well.

8   Stir in the prepared fruit and almonds.

9   Tip the mixture into the prepared tin, pushing it down and smoothing the top. Place the prepared parchment square over the cake tin with the folded flaps pointing down to loosely cover the cake when it goes into the oven.

10 Bake for 2–2¼ hours. Leave the cake to cool in the tin for 12 hours.

Continued overleaf →

Christmas Cake continued

FOR THE ICING:

11 Warm the apricot jam and spread it over the cold cake.

12 Lightly dust the work surface with icing sugar and roll the marzipan into a 30cm/12 inch circle. Carefully lift the marzipan onto the cake, pressing and shaping it to cover the cake. Use your hands or a cake smoother. Trim away any excess marzipan and leave the cake for at least 12 hours for the marzipan to set. Either proceed to the next step or wrap the cake tightly in kitchen foil and store it in a tin until a few days before you plan to serve it.

13 Roll the fondant icing into a large circle. Carefully lift it over the marzipan, pressing and shaping it with a cake smoother to cover the cake. Trim away any excess. To store the cake, wrap it in parchment and a double layer of kitchen foil before storing it in an airtight container where it will keep for several weeks.

FOR THE CRYSTALISED CRANBERRY AND ROSEMARY DECORATION:

14 Measure the caster sugar into a bowl and cover a large chopping board with baking parchment.

15 Scatter the granulated sugar over the base of a saucepan and sprinkle the water evenly over the sugar. Put the saucepan over a medium heat until bubbles start to appear. Shake the pan, but do not stir, and leave it to simmer gently until the sugar is fully dissolved. Remove the pan of clear syrup from the heat.

16 Carefully slide a few rosemary fronds into the hot syrup. Turn the herbs in the syrup so that they are fully coated. Using tongs, lift up the rosemary, one piece at a time, and allow excess syrup to drain off. Transfer the herbs to the bowl of caster sugar and turn them over so they are well covered in sugar. Lift the sugared herbs onto the baking parchment and spread out the herb leaves if required. Dust a little caster sugar over the herbs and leave them to dry.

17 Repeat the frosting process with the cranberries.

18 When completely dry, place the frosted rosemary fronds and cranberries on top of your iced cake.

CHAPTER 2

Biscuits, Scones & Traybakes

Popular bakes for sharing and
keeping – these teatime treats
really are gluten free!

Chocolate Chip Cookies

These delicious gluten free cookies are the perfect accompaniment to a cup of tea! This quick and easy recipe makes 12–16 cookies.

MAKES: 12–16
COOKING TIME: 18–20 MINUTES

200g FREEE Plain White Flour
150g sugar
½ tsp FREEE Bicarbonate
  of Soda
½ tsp FREEE Xanthan Gum
pinch of salt
1 egg
50ml oil, plus extra for tray
1 tbsp vanilla extract
75g dark chocolate chips

1 Preheat the oven to 180°C, Fan 160°C, 350°F, Gas 4. Rub some oil around the inside of 2 baking trays or insert a baking liner.

2 Measure the flour, sugar, bicarbonate of soda, xanthan gum and salt into a bowl and stir well to combine. Sift everything into a mixing bowl.

3 Break the egg into the bowl, pour in the oil and vanilla and mix really well.

4 Using your hands, gather everything together into a dry dough.

5 Add the chocolate chips and work them into the dough with your fingers.

6 Spoon 6–8 piles of dough onto each prepared baking tray leaving space around each mound of dough. Push any chips that fall out back into the dough.

7 Bake for 18–20 minutes until the cookies are light brown on the edges and still slightly soft in the middle. Leave to cool on the trays for 5 minutes, then transfer the cookies to a wire rack to cool completely.

Shortbread Finger Biscuits

The initial mixing and resting stages are the key to creating the delicious buttery crunch of these gluten free shortbread finger biscuits. The recipe makes 12 classic shortbread fingers.

MAKES: 12
COOKING TIME: 45 MINUTES

200g FREEE Plain
    White Flour
1 tsp FREEE Xanthan Gum
75g caster sugar
pinch of salt
2 tsp water
150g butter, plus extra for
    baking tray

1   Rub some butter around the inside of a 15 x 20cm/6 x 8 inch baking tray or insert a baking liner and preheat the oven to 200°C, Fan 180°C, 400°F, Gas 6.

2   Put the flour and xanthan gum into a bowl, stir to combine and sift into a kitchen blender.

3   Add the sugar and salt and pulse to mix. Add the water and pulse again.

4   Cover and leave it to rest for 20 minutes.

5   Chop the butter into cubes, add this to the bowl and pulse until the dough holds together.

6   Tip the mixture into the prepared baking tray, pressing it into the corners and smoothing the top.

7   Bake for 20 minutes.

8   Remove the tray from the oven and carefully cut the shortbread into 12 rectangles. Press a fork into each rectangle slice three times.

9   Return the shortbread to the oven and bake for a further 22–25 minutes. Leave the shortbread to cool in the baking tray. Store the cool biscuits in an airtight tin.

Sponge Finger Biscuits

Sometimes called Savoiardi Biscuits, Naples Biscuits and Lady Fingers, these crisp and light finger-shaped biscuits are perfect in creamy desserts such as trifle and tiramisu.

MAKES: 15–18
COOKING TIME: 40–45 MINUTES

oil, for baking tray
50g FREEE Plain White Flour
25g FREEE Cornflour
25g icing sugar
2 eggs
¼ tsp vitamin C
25g caster sugar, plus extra
  for dusting
¼ tsp vanilla extract

1 Preheat the oven to 150°C, Fan 130°C, 300°F, Gas 2. Rub some oil around the inside of a 12-hole éclair or sponge finger baking tray, or around the inside of a large baking tray or insert a baking liner.

2 Measure the plain flour and cornflour into a bowl, stir to combine, then sift into another bowl. Sift the icing sugar into a bowl.

3 Break the eggs, separating the yolks into one mixing bowl and whites into another mixing bowl.

4 Add the vitamin C to the whites and beat until stiff. Continue beating as you add the icing sugar, a spoon at a time.

5 Add the caster sugar and vanilla to the yolks and beat until the mixture thickens slightly.

6 Using a large metal spoon, take 2 spoons of beaten egg white and mix it into the yolks using a cutting and folding action.

7 Add the remaining egg whites, a couple of spoons at a time, using the spoon to fold it in, without knocking out the air.

8 Sift one-third of the flour blend over the top and mix gently with the spoon in the cutting and folding action. Sift the flour into the bowl in two more stages, continuing the gentle cutting and folding action.

9 Spoon or pipe the mixture into the holes of the sponge finger tray, or spoon or pipe sausage shapes onto a baking tray. Working quickly, sprinkle a large pinch of caster sugar over each sponge finger.

10 Bake immediately for 40–45 minutes. Remove from the oven and leave on the baking tray for a few minutes. Transfer the fingers to a cooling rack.

11 When cold, store in an airtight tin.

Rice Flour Vanilla Cookies

If you like vanilla, you'll love these cookies. These gluten free treats are the perfect accompaniment to a cup of tea or coffee, and the recipe can easily be made vegan by following our ingredient swaps. Makes 24–30 cookies.

OPTION:

MAKES: 24–30
COOKING TIME: 20–22 MINUTES

oil, for baking tray
100g FREEE Rice Flour
1 tsp FREEE Baking Powder
75g butter or plant butter
75g caster sugar
1 tbsp milk or plant milk
2 tsp vanilla extract
4 tsp water

1   Preheat the oven to 190°C, Fan 170°C, 375°F, Gas 5. Rub some oil around the inside of a large baking tray or insert a baking liner.

2   Put the flour and baking powder into a bowl and stir to combine.

3   Cut the butter into small cubes and put them into a mixing bowl. Add the sugar and beat until smooth.

4   Beat in the milk and vanilla.

5   Add the prepared flour and mix well.

6   Stir in the water to make a soft dough. If very soft, chill the dough for 10 minutes. Divide the mixture into 24–30 pieces and roll each one into a ball. Transfer the dough balls to the prepared baking tray, flattening them slightly.

7   Bake for 20–22 minutes.

8   Leave to cool on the tray for 5 minutes then transfer to a rack to cool. Store the cold biscuits in an airtight tin.

Rice Flour Peanut Butter Cookies

Rice flour adds a pleasing crunch to these family favourite cookies. You can use smooth or crunchy peanut butter or a combination of the two. This recipe makes about 24 cookies, which will keep best in an airtight tin.

MAKES: 24
COOKING TIME: 15–20 MINUTES

oil, for baking tray
175g FREEE Rice Flour
1 tsp FREEE Baking Powder
250g smooth or crunchy
    peanut butter
175g soft brown sugar
1 egg
3 tbsp water

1   Preheat the oven to 180°C, Fan 160°C, 350°F, Gas 4. Rub some oil around the inside of 2 baking trays or insert a baking liner.

2   Measure the flour and baking powder into a bowl and stir to combine.

3   Put the peanut butter and sugar into another bowl and beat them together.

4   Beat in the egg and water.

5   Sift the prepared flour into the bowl and stir to form a ball of cookie dough.

6   Take teaspoons of dough, rolling each into a small ball. Place the dough balls on the prepared baking trays and flatten the dough slightly with the back of a fork.

7   Bake for 15–20 minutes until golden.

8   Leave to cool on the tray for 5 minutes then transfer to a rack to cool. Store the cold biscuits in an airtight tin.

Gingerbread People

Get the kids involved with this easy, gluten free recipe to make 6 large or more smaller gingerbread people. You will find the smell hard to resist while baking!

200g FREEE Plain White
 Flour, plus extra for dusting
1 tsp ground ginger
½ tsp ground cinnamon
½ tsp FREEE Xanthan Gum
¼ tsp FREEE Bicarbonate
 of Soda
75g caster sugar
50g butter, plus extra for
 baking trays
2 tbsp golden syrup
1 egg
writing icing, to decorate

1   Measure the flour, ginger, cinnamon, xanthan gum and bicarbonate of soda into a mixing bowl and stir to combine. Sift the flour blend into a separate large mixing bowl.

2   Put the sugar, butter and golden syrup into a saucepan and heat gently, swirling the pan occasionally until dissolved.

3   Pour the saucepan contents onto the prepared flour and stir to combine.

4   Add the egg and mix into a sticky dough. Cover and chill the dough for 1 hour or until firm.

5   Preheat the oven to 180°C, Fan 160°C, 350°F, Gas 4. Rub some butter around the inside of 2 large baking trays or insert a baking liner.

6   Dust the work surface with flour, put the dough in the middle and sprinkle it with more flour. Roll out the dough until 7mm/ ¼ inch thick. Press the gingerbread people cookie cutter into the dough to cut out the shapes. Gently transfer the shapes to the prepared baking trays, leaving plenty of space between each shape.

7   Gather leftover dough into a ball, roll it out again and cut more shapes.

8   Bake for 10–12 minutes. Leave to cool on the tray.

9   Using writing icing, decorate the cold gingerbread people however you wish.

← Image on previous page

Lemon Drizzle Traybake

This lemon drizzle cake is cooked as a traybake so that it can be cut into portion sizes. Stored in a tin or wrapped in kitchen foil, this cake will keep well for several days. For a special treat, gently warm the cake and serve it with mascarpone or double cream.

MAKES: 12–15
COOKING TIME: 25–30 MINUTES

150g butter, plus extra for baking tray
150g caster sugar
1 tbsp finely grated lemon rind
3 eggs
175g FREEE Self Raising White Flour

DRIZZLE:
75ml lemon juice
75g granulated sugar

ICING:
2 tbsp icing sugar
½ tsp lemon juice

1   Preheat the oven to 180°C, Fan 160°C, 350°F, Gas 4. Rub some butter around the inside of a 15 x 20cm/6 x 8 inch baking tray or insert a cake liner.

2   Cut the butter into small cubes and put them into a mixing bowl. Add the sugar and beat together until light and fluffy.

3   Add the lemon rind to the bowl and stir to combine.

4   Break the eggs into the bowl one at a time, ensuring each is well incorporated before adding the next.

5   Sift the flour into the bowl and stir it into the mixture.

6   Tip the mixture into the prepared baking tray, spreading it into the corners.

7   Bake for 25–30 minutes. Leave the traybake in its tin.

FOR THE DRIZZLE:

8   Put the lemon juice and granulated sugar into a saucepan over a medium heat and stir until the sugar is dissolved and a syrup has formed.

9   Prick the surface of the cake with a skewer or cocktail stick. Pour the syrup slowly all over the top of the warm cake and leave to cool completely. When cold, cut into small squares.

FOR THE ICING:

10 Put the icing sugar into a bowl and add the lemon juice. Stir to make an icing. Take a teaspoon of icing and dribble it over the cake in a zigzag fashion.

Chocolate Chip Biscotti

Serve biscotti with a cup of coffee or to accompany ice cream or creamy mousse. This recipe will make 16–18 lovely crunchy biscuits which will keep well in an airtight tin. You can use milk or plain chocolate chips.

MAKES: 16–18
COOKING TIME: 25 MINUTES + 7 MINUTES + 7 MINUTES

oil, for baking tray
125g FREEE Plain White Flour, plus extra for dusting
¼ tsp FREEE Bicarbonate of Soda
⅛ tsp FREEE Xanthan Gum
75g caster sugar
25g ground almonds
75g chocolate chips
1 egg
1 tbsp vanilla extract

1 Preheat the oven to 180°C, Fan 160°C, 350°F, Gas 4. Rub some oil around the inside of a large baking tray or insert a baking liner.

2 Measure the flour, bicarbonate of soda and xanthan gum into a mixing bowl, stir to combine and sift into a mixing bowl.

3 Add the sugar, ground almonds and chocolate chips and stir to mix.

4 Break the egg into another bowl, add the vanilla and beat them together.

5 Pour the mixture into the mixing bowl and stir into a soft, slightly sticky, dough.

6 Dust the dough with flour and transfer it to the prepared tray. Using your hands, shape the dough into a flat 7.5 x 20cm/ 3 x 8 inch rectangle.

7 Bake for 25 minutes. Remove from the oven and leave to cool.

8 Cut the cooked biscotti dough into 1cm/⅜ inch thick slices. Lay out the slices on the baking tray.

9 Bake for 7 minutes then turn the biscotti over and bake for a further 7 minutes. Transfer to a wire rack to cool completely. Store the cold biscotti in an airtight container.

Almond and Cranberry Traybake

This super traybake has a cranberry layer sandwiched between two different almond layers.

MAKES: 12
COOKING TIME: 40–45 MINUTES

CRANBERRY FILLING:
175g dried cranberries
150g granulated sugar
1 orange

ALMOND SPONGE BASE LAYER:
200g FREEE Plain
   White Flour
100g soft brown sugar
¼ tsp FREEE Xanthan Gum
75g ground almonds
75g butter, plus extra for
   baking tray
1 egg

ALMOND AND CRANBERRY
TOPPING:
2 eggs
100g caster sugar
50g FREEE Self Raising
   White Flour
75g flaked almonds
50g dried cranberries
orange rind strips, set aside
   from filling
1 tbsp demerara sugar

FOR THE CRANBERRY FILLING:

1   To make the cranberry filling, put the cranberries and sugar into a saucepan. Peel off strips of orange rind, cover and set these aside for the topping. Squeeze the orange juice into a jug and add water to make 150ml of liquid. Put the pan over a gentle heat, bring to the boil and simmer gently for 3 minutes.

2   Remove from the heat and, using a stick blender, purée the cranberries. Cover and set aside.

FOR THE ALMOND SPONGE BASE LAYER:

3   Preheat the oven to 180°C, Fan 160°C, 350°F, Gas 4. Rub butter around the inside of a 23 x 33cm/9 x 13 inch baking tray or insert a baking liner.

4   Measure the plain flour, soft brown sugar and xanthan gum into a bowl, stir to combine and sift into a mixing bowl.

5   Stir in the ground almonds.

6   Chop the butter into small cubes, add them to the bowl and, using a fork or pastry blender, work it in until it resembles breadcrumbs.

7   Add the egg and mix thoroughly to moisten the mixture.

8   Tip the mixture into the baking tray, pressing it into a flat dough. Spoon the cranberry filling onto the pastry and spread it out evenly.

FOR THE ALMOND AND CRANBERRY TOPPING:

9   Break two eggs into a bowl, add the caster sugar and beat together well. Sift the flour over the top and mix again. Pour the mixture all over the cranberry layer.

10   Sprinkle flaked almonds evenly over the top. Dice the cranberries and scatter them over the almonds. Scatter the reserved orange rind strips and demerara sugar over the traybake.

11   Bake for 40–45 minutes. Leave to cool in the tray and cut into squares or rectangles when cool. Store the slices in a tin.

Flapjacks

   OPTION:

Flapjacks are a classic traybake made with oats. If you don't have demerara sugar to hand, you can use coconut sugar, muscovado or soft brown sugar.

MAKES: 12
COOKING TIME: 45–50 MINUTES

150g butter or plant butter,
   plus extra for baking tray
75g golden syrup
75g demerara sugar
250g FREEE Porridge Oats

1 Preheat the oven to 150°C, Fan 130°C, 300°F, Gas 2. Rub a little butter around the inside of a 20cm/8 inch square baking tray.

2 Put the butter, golden syrup and sugar into a saucepan and heat gently, stirring occasionally, until the sugar has completely dissolved.

3 Remove from the heat, add the oats and stir to combine.

4 Tip the mixture into the prepared tray and smooth the top.

5 Bake for 45–50 minutes. Remove from the oven and, while still warm, cut into slices and leave to cool completely.

6 When cold, slice again and remove from the dish. Store the flapjack slices in an airtight tin.

Oat and Date Slices

   OPTION:

The naturally sweet date layer baked into the middle of these slices provides the perfect treat between two crumbly, crunchy, oaty, layers.

MAKES: 12
COOKING TIME: 45–50 MINUTES

200g dates
1 tsp lemon rind
¼ tsp FREEE Bicarbonate
   of Soda
200ml water
175g butter or plant butter,
   plus extra for baking tray
100g FREEE Self Raising
   White Flour
125g soft brown sugar
200g FREEE Porridge Oats

1 Roughly chop the dates into a saucepan. Add the lemon rind and sprinkle the bicarbonate of soda over the top. Add the water and put over a gentle heat. Gently simmer for 3 minutes, then remove from the heat.

2 Preheat the oven to 180°C, Fan 160°C, 350°F, Gas 4. Rub a little butter around the inside of a 20cm/8 inch square baking tray.

3 Chop the butter into small cubes and put them in a mixing bowl. Add the flour and brown sugar. Using a fork, mix until it resembles coarse breadcrumbs. Add the oats and stir to combine.

4 Transfer half the mixture into the prepared tray, spread it out evenly and press flat.

5 Mash the dates with a fork and spread them over the oat base. Spread the remaining oat mixture over the dates and press flat again.

6 Bake for 40–45 minutes. Remove from the oven and leave in the tray to cool completely .

7 When cold, slice into squares or slices. Store the oat and date slices in an airtight tin.

Chocolate Brownies

When you make these delicious chocolate brownies nobody will guess that they are gluten free! This has been one of our most often requested gluten free recipes, which first appeared on our flour packets back in 2000. For brownies that are squishy in the middle, use a short cooking time; for firmer brownies, simply cook for longer. Then cut the traybake into 12 or 16 squares or rectangles.

MAKES: 12–16
COOKING TIME: 22–30 MINUTES

150g dark chocolate
100g butter, plus extra for
    baking dish
200g sugar
100g FREEE Plain White Flour
1 tsp FREEE Baking Powder
3 eggs

1   Preheat the oven to 180°C, Fan 160°C, 350°F, Gas 4. Rub some butter around the inside of a 15 x 20cm/6 x 8 inch baking dish or insert a baking liner.

2   Gently melt together the chocolate and butter.

3   In a bowl, mix the sugar, flour and baking powder.

4   Break the eggs into a large bowl, beat to combine then beat in the flour mix.

5   Stir in the melted chocolate and butter.

6   Pour into the prepared dish.

7   Bake for 22-30 minutes.

8   Cut into squares or slices before serving warm or cold.

CHAPTER 3

Bread

Nothing beats fresh home-made bread, and with the right recipes and flours, gluten free bread is no exception. Sandwich loaves, rolls, flatbreads and more.

White Bread

Kneading is not necessary in this white bread recipe which uses a batter method. For a vegan version, swap gram flour and water for the egg whites.

OPTION:

MAKES: 1 LOAF
COOKING TIME: 55–60 MINUTES

2 egg whites (or 20g FREEE Gram Flour mixed with 40ml water)
2 tbsp sugar
1 tsp salt
6 tbsp oil, plus extra for tin
1 tsp vinegar
425ml water
500g FREEE White Bread Flour
2 tsp quick yeast

1   Rub some oil around the inside of a 900g (2lb) bread tin.

2   Put the egg whites (or gram flour and water), sugar, salt, 3 tablespoons of the oil, the vinegar and water into a bowl and whisk together.

3   Add the flour and yeast, then whisk to a smooth, thick batter.

4   Drizzle the remaining 3 tablespoons of oil over the sticky batter and, using a spatula, turn the mixture a couple of times in the bowl to encourage the formation of a doughy mass.

5   Tip the dough into the prepared tin and smooth the top. Invert a large mixing bowl over the tin and leave until the dough has risen to 7mm/¼ inch below the top of the tin, about 60–90 minutes.

6   Preheat the oven to 220°C, Fan 200°C, 425°F, Gas 7.

7   Bake for 55–60 minutes.

8   Turn out the cooked loaf to cool on a wire rack.

9   Allow the bread to cool completely before slicing.

White Bread Rolls

Bake these useful white bread rolls for lunchboxes or picnics or freeze them as a handy standby. This recipe makes 8 small rolls, for more rolls double all of the ingredients.

MAKES: 8
COOKING TIME: 15–20 MINUTES

1 egg white
2 tsp sugar
¼ tsp salt
2 tbsp oil, plus extra for tin
½ tsp vinegar
200ml milk
250g FREEE White Bread
    Flour, plus extra for dusting
2 tsp quick yeast

1   Rub some oil around the inside of 8 Yorkshire or muffin tin holes.

2   Put the egg white, sugar, salt, 1 tablespoon of the oil, the vinegar and milk into a bowl and whisk well.

3   Add the flour and yeast, then mix into a smooth thick batter.

4   Cover with an upturned bowl and leave in a warm place until doubled in size, about 1–2 hours.

5   Sprinkle the remaining tablespoon of oil over the batter and use a spatula to turn the mixture a couple of times in the bowl to form an oily, doughy mass.

6   Divide the doughy mass between the holes of the Yorkshire or muffin tin. Cover loosely with a clean tea towel and leave to rise for 35–40 minutes.

7   Preheat the oven to 200°C, Fan 180°C, 400°F, Gas 6.

8   Sprinkle some flour over the top of the rolls and bake for 15–20 minutes. Transfer the rolls to a wire rack to cool.

9   Allow the rolls to cool completely before slicing.

Brown Bread Rolls

This recipe makes 8 small brown bread rolls, which are best gently reheated before serving at breakfast, lunch or supper. Wrap and freeze any rolls not eaten on the baking day so they can be enjoyed on another occasion. Alternatively, you may like to try the White Bread Rolls on page 121.

MAKES: 8
COOKING TIME: 15–20 MINUTES

1 egg white
2 tsp sugar
¼ tsp salt
2 tbsp oil, plus extra for tin
½ tsp vinegar
200ml milk
250g FREEE Brown Bread Flour, plus extra for dusting
2 tsp quick yeast

1 Rub some oil around the inside of 8 Yorkshire or muffin tin holes.

2 Put the egg white, sugar, salt, 1 tablespoon of the oil, the vinegar and milk into a bowl and whisk well.

3 Add the flour and yeast, then mix into a smooth, thick batter.

4 Cover with an upturned bowl and leave in a warm place until doubled in size, about 1–2 hours.

5 Sprinkle the last tablespoon of oil over the batter and use a spatula to turn the mixture a couple of times in the bowl, to form an oily, doughy mass.

6 Divide the doughy mass between the holes of the Yorkshire or muffin tin. Cover loosely with a clean tea towel and leave to rise for 35–40 minutes.

7 Preheat the oven to 200°C, Fan 180°C, 400°F, Gas 6.

8 Sprinkle some flour over the top of the rolls and bake for 15–20 minutes.

9 Transfer the rolls to a wire rack to cool. Allow the rolls to cool completely before slicing.

10 Reheat the rolls for a couple of minutes before serving.

All-in-One Bread Loaf

A simple gluten free bread loaf made with
FREEE Plain White Flour and Xanthan Gum.
This loaf has an open crumpet crumb structure
and is delicious toasted.

MAKES: 1 LOAF
COOKING TIME: 50–55 MINUTES

500g FREEE Plain White
   Flour
2 tsp FREEE Xanthan Gum
1 tsp quick yeast
1 tsp sugar
1 tsp salt
500ml tepid water
3 tbsp oil, plus extra for tin

1 Preheat the oven to 220°C, Fan 200°C, 425°F, Gas 7. Rub some oil around the inside of a 900g (2lb) bread tin.

2 Put the flour, xanthan gum, yeast, sugar and salt into a large mixing bowl and mix well.

3 Add the water followed by 2 tablespoons of the oil. Sprinkle the last tablespoon of oil over the batter. Run a spatula around the outside of the bowl and turn the mixture to form a sticky mass.

4 Tip the sticky mass into the prepared tin and smooth the top. Invert a mixing bowl over the tin and leave until the dough has risen to 7mm/¼ inch below the top of the tin, about 60–90 minutes.

5 Bake for 50–55 minutes.

6 Turn the bread out of the tin and leave to cool on a wire rack. Allow the bread to cool completely before slicing.

Air Fryer Mini White Bread Loaves

Five or six mini silicone moulds, rectangular, square or round, are essential for making these tasty gluten free mini bread loaves, which can be ready to eat in under an hour.

MAKES: 5–6
COOKING TIME: 11 MINUTES

1 egg white
2 tbsp oil, plus extra for tin
2 tsp sugar
½ tsp salt
½ tsp vinegar
150ml milk
125g FREEE White Bread Flour
1 tsp quick yeast

1 Check how the mini silicone loaf cases will fit in your air fryer, allowing space for the air to circulate.

2 Put the egg white into a mixing bowl. Add the oil, sugar, salt and vinegar and whisk together well.

3 Add the milk to the bowl and whisk again.

4 Add the flour and mix into a smooth batter.

5 Finally, add the yeast and whisk well.

6 Divide the batter between the silicone moulds, filling them no more than three-quarters full. Set the air fryer to 200°C/400°F and run for 5 minutes. Working quickly, open the warm air fryer and lift the silicone moulds into the machine, then close the door. Leave the dough to rise in the machine for 30 minutes.

7 Without opening the door, set the air fryer to 200°C/400°F and bake for 11 minutes.

8 Carefully remove the mini loaves from the machine and leave them to cool on a wire rack. When completely cold, remove the mini loaves from their moulds.

Brown Soda Bread

This versatile bread can be made with either FREEE Brown Bread Flour or FREEE White Bread Flour. Happy baking and eating!

MAKES: 1 LOAF
COOKING TIME: 60 MINUTES, PLUS 5–10 MINUTES

500g FREEE Brown Bread Flour
2 tsp FREEE Bicarbonate of Soda
½ tbsp sugar
¼ tsp salt
250ml tepid water
3 tbsp oil, plus extra for tin
200ml natural yoghurt
1 tbsp lemon juice

1   Preheat the oven to 240°C, Fan 220°C, 475°F, Gas 9. Rub some oil around a 900g (2lb) loaf tin or insert a baking liner.

2   Put the flour, bicarbonate of soda, sugar and salt into a bowl, stir to combine and sift into a large mixing bowl.

3   Add half the water and 2 tablespoons of the oil and, using a fork, mix into even-sized breadcrumbs.

4   Put the remaining water into another bowl, add the yoghurt and lemon juice and mix well.

5   Pour into the mixing bowl and stir until everything is combined and forms a thick batter.

6   Drizzle the remaining tablespoon of oil over the batter. Using a spatula, turn the mixture a couple of times in the bowl.

7   Tip the batter into the prepared tin and smooth the top. Brush some oil over a piece of kitchen foil. With the oiled side down, cover the tin, creating a dome so the bread can rise during cooking. Bake for 60 minutes.

8   Carefully remove the kitchen foil, reduce the temperature to 200°C, Fan 180°C, 400°F, Gas 6 and bake for a further 5–10 minutes. The bottom should sound hollow when tapped.

9   Turn the loaf out onto a wire rack to cool. Allow the bread to cool completely before slicing.

Ciabatta

Here is our gluten free version of ciabatta,
an Italian-style slipper loaf.

MAKES: 1 LOAF
COOKING TIME: 35 MINUTES,
PLUS 7–8 MINUTES

300g FREEE White
    Bread Flour
2 tbsp FREEE Gram Flour
1 tsp quick yeast
½ tsp sugar
250ml tepid water
½ tsp salt
2 tbsp olive oil, plus extra
    for tin

1   Put the white bread flour, gram flour, yeast and sugar into a
    mixing bowl and blend them together.

2   Pour the water into the bowl and stir to combine.

3   Sprinkle the salt over the top and beat well.

4   Add 1 tablespoon of the oil and stir the batter.

5   Invert a large bowl over the batter and leave to rest in a warm
    place until risen, about 90 minutes.

6   Rub some oil around the inside of a large baking tray or insert
    a baking liner.

7   Sprinkle the remaining tablespoon of oil over the dough. Using
    a spatula, gently scrape around the edge of the swollen batter
    and ease it onto the baking tray. Gently shape the swollen
    batter into a 23 x 10cm/9 x 4 inch oval. Invert a large bowl
    over the oval and leave in a warm place to rise for 30 minutes.

8   Twenty minutes before you are going to bake, preheat the
    oven to 240°C, Fan 220°C, 475°F, Gas 9. Remove the inverted
    bowl and bake for 35 minutes. Leave to cool on a wire rack
    before eating.

9   Before serving the ciabatta, preheat the oven to 240°C, Fan 220°C,
    475°F, Gas 9 and bake for 7–8 minutes. Slice and serve warm.

Sun-dried Tomato Bread

Studded with sweet nuggets of sun-dried tomatoes, this loaf is a delicious complement to any meal and a great picnic loaf. Serve slices on their own or toasted.

MAKES: 1 LOAF
COOKING TIME: 45–50 MINUTES

1 egg white
2 tsp sugar
1 tsp salt
3 tbsp oil, plus extra for tin
1 tbsp vinegar
175ml water
250g FREEE White Bread Flour
2 tsp quick yeast
50g sun-dried tomatoes in oil
1 tsp dried oregano
1 tsp dried basil

1   Rub some oil around the inside of a 450g (1lb) loaf tin or insert a loaf liner.

2   Put the egg white, sugar, salt, 2 tablespoons of the oil, the vinegar and water into a bowl and whisk together well.

3   Add the flour and yeast, mixing to a smooth, thick batter.

4   Chop the tomatoes into chunks, then add to the bowl with the oregano and basil. Stir to combine.

5   Sprinkle the remaining tablespoon of oil over the batter and use a spatula to turn the mixture a couple of times in the bowl to form an oily, doughy mass.

6   Tip the doughy mass into the prepared tin and smooth the top. Invert a large mixing bowl over the tin and leave until the dough has risen to 7mm/¼ inch below the top of the tin, about 60-90 minutes.

7   Preheat the oven to 220°C, Fan 200°C, 425°F, Gas 7.

8   Remove the upturned bowl and bake for 45–50 minutes.

9   Turn out onto a wire rack to cool. Allow the bread to cool completely before slicing.

Seeded Brown Bread

Bake this recipe with egg white or follow our gram flour swap for a vegan version. Linseeds, caraway or sesame seeds can also be used instead of the seeds suggested below.

OPTION:

MAKES: 1 LOAF
COOKING TIME: 55–60 MINUTES

2 egg whites (or 20g FREEE Gram Flour mixed with 40ml water)
1 tbsp sugar
1 tsp salt
6 tbsp oil, plus extra for tin
1 tsp vinegar
530ml tepid water
500g FREEE Brown Bread Flour
2 tsp quick yeast
2 tbsp pumpkin seeds
2 tbsp sunflower seeds
2 tbsp poppy seeds

1 Rub some oil around the inside of a 900g (2lb) bread tin.

2 Put the egg whites (or gram flour and water), sugar, salt, 3 tablespoons of the oil, the vinegar and water into a bowl and whisk together.

3 Add the flour and yeast, then whisk to a smooth, thick batter. Stir in the seeds.

4 Drizzle the remaining 3 tablespoons of oil over the batter and, using a spatula, turn the mixture a couple of times in the bowl to encourage the formation of a doughy mass.

5 Tip the dough into the prepared bread tin and smooth the top. Invert a large mixing bowl over the tin and leave until the dough has risen to 7mm/¼ inch below the top of the tin, about 60-90 minutes.

6 Preheat the oven to 220°C, Fan 200°C, 425°F, Gas 7.

7 Bake for 55-60 minutes.

8 Turn out onto a wire rack to cool.

9 Allow the bread to cool completely before slicing.

Spiced Brown Fruit Loaf

This fruited brown loaf is delicious on its own or toasted and spread with butter. Slices of the bread will freeze well and can be toasted from frozen for breakfast or tea time.

MAKES: 1 LOAF
COOKING TIME: 40–45 MINUTES

50g butter
25g dried cranberries
50g currants
25g pumpkin seeds
2 egg whites
50g dark soft brown sugar
½ tsp salt
1 tsp vinegar
450ml milk
400g FREEE Brown
    Bread Flour
2 tsp ground cinnamon
2 tsp quick yeast
1 tbsp oil, plus extra for tin

1   Rub some oil around the inside of a 900g (2lb) bread tin or insert a baking liner.

2   Gently melt the butter and measure the cranberries, currants and pumpkin seeds into a small bowl.

3   Put the egg whites into a mixing bowl, add the sugar, salt and vinegar, and whisk together well.

4   Add the milk and melted butter and whisk again.

5   Sift the flour and cinnamon into the bowl and tip any bran left in the sieve into the bowl.

6   Sprinkle the yeast over the top and stir everything into a smooth, thick batter.

7   Tip the bowl of fruit and seeds into the mixing bowl and stir to combine.

8   Drizzle the oil over the batter and, using a spatula, turn the mixture a couple of times in the bowl to encourage the formation of a doughy mass.

9   Tip the dough into the prepared tin and smooth the top. Invert a large mixing bowl over the tin and leave until the dough has risen to 7mm/¼ inch below the top of the tin, about 60–90 minutes.

10 Preheat the oven to 220°C, Fan 200°C, 425°F, Gas 7.

11 Bake for 40–45 minutes.

12 Turn the loaf out of the tin and leave to cool on a wire rack.

13 Allow the bread to cool completely before slicing

CHAPTER 4

Yorkshire Puddings, Pancakes & Doughnuts

Batters for Yorkshire pudding,
traditional sweet pancakes, super
savoury pancakes and gluten free
ring doughnuts.

Yorkshire Puddings

The traditional accompaniment to a roast lunch is Yorkshire Pudding. This gluten free version, which makes 12 small puddings or 1 large, can be a great-tasting addition to your meal that the whole family can enjoy. For best results, preheat your metal baking tray, and a very hot oven is essential.

MAKES: 12 SMALL OR 1 LARGE
COOKING TIME: SMALLER
PUDDINGS 25–30 MINUTES;
LARGER PUDDING 35–45
MINUTES

oil, for baking tray
60g FREEE Cornflour
40g FREEE Plain White Flour
¼ tsp salt
¼ tsp pepper
2 eggs
160ml milk

1 Preheat the oven to 220°C, Fan 200°C, 425°F, Gas 7. Put a teaspoon of oil into each hole of a 12-hole muffin tray or 2 tablespoons into a large baking tray.

2 When the oven is hot, put the muffin or baking tray into the oven until the fat is very hot and bubbling.

3 Measure the cornflour, flour, salt and pepper into a mixing bowl, stir to combine and sift them into another bowl or jug.

4 Add the eggs and milk and beat into a smooth batter.

5 Carefully remove the muffin tray or baking tray from the oven. Working quickly, divide the batter between the muffin tray holes or pour it into the large baking tray.

6 Return the baking tray to the oven and bake smaller puddings for 25-30 minutes and larger ones for up to 35-45 minutes, depending on your preference for crispness of the pudding.

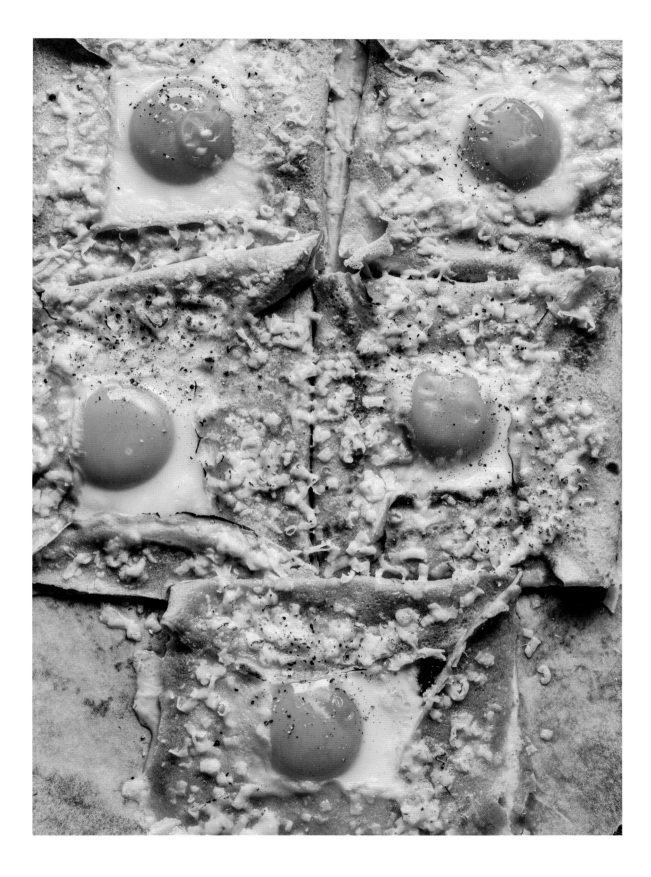

American-style Pancakes

These thick, fluffy pancakes are the perfect Sunday brunch treat. They can be made free from allergens using our clever ingredient swaps. These pancakes are delicious and wholesome topped with banana and chopped almonds, then drizzled with maple syrup.

OPTION:

MAKES: 10
COOKING TIME: 2–5 MINUTES PER PANCAKE

250g FREEE Plain White Flour
2 tbsp icing sugar
1¾ tbsp FREEE Baking Powder
2 eggs (or 2 tbsp FREEE
   Gram Flour mixed with
   4 tbsp water)
150ml milk or plant milk
50g butter or plant butter,
   melted
oil, for frying

TO SERVE, OPTIONAL:
sliced banana
chopped almonds
maple syrup

1 Put the flour, icing sugar and baking powder into a bowl and stir to combine.

2 Break the eggs into a mixing bowl (or measure the gram flour and water into the bowl). Add the milk and beat together well.

3 Stir in the dry ingredients, then add the melted butter. Beat into a smooth, thick batter.

4 Pour a little oil into a frying pan, roll it around to cover the surface and heat until nice and hot.

5 Pour batter into the pan to make 7.5cm/3 inch circles and cook over a medium heat. When bubbles appear on the surface and the base is golden, turn the pancakes over and cook the other side.

6 Transfer the cooked pancakes to a plate and repeat with the remaining batter.

7 Serve warm with your favourite toppings.

Buckwheat Blinis with Smoked Salmon and Cream Cheese

Great for serving with drinks, at a buffet lunch and as party food. This recipe will make about 50 of these little, buckwheat flour canapé pancakes which can be cooked in advance, wrapped in foil and frozen. When required, thaw and assemble with crème fraîche and smoked salmon. Alternatively, for a dairy free option, serve them with a hummus and sliced red pepper topping.

OPTION:

MAKES: 50
COOKING TIME: 2–5 MINUTES PER PANCAKE

75g FREEE Buckwheat Flour
1 tsp FREEE Baking Powder
1 egg
150ml milk or plant milk
oil, for frying

TOPPING:
100g smoked salmon offcuts
100g full-fat cream cheese
1 tsp natural yoghurt
salt and pepper
fresh dill sprigs, to garnish

1 Put the flour and baking powder into a bowl, stir to combine and sift into a mixing bowl or jug.

2 Add the egg and half the milk and beat into a smooth paste.

3 Beat in the remaining milk.

4 Put a little oil into a large frying pan, roll it around to cover the surface and heat until the pan is nice and hot.

5 Drop teaspoons of batter onto the pan to make small blinis. When bubbles appear on the surface of the blini and the base is golden, turn it over and cook the other side. Transfer the cooked blinis to a cooling rack.

6 Repeat with the remaining batter.

FOR THE TOPPING:
7 Chop the smoked salmon into a bowl. Add the cream cheese and yoghurt and stir to combine. Divide the mixture between the cold blinis. Season with salt and pepper as required.

8 Put a sprig of dill on the top of each blini before serving.

Dosa with Curry and Chutney

Dosa have Southern Indian heritage and make a great vegan accompaniment to any curry.

MAKES: 8
COOKING TIME: 2–5 MINUTES PER DOSA

COCONUT CHUTNEY:
2cm piece of fresh ginger
1 tbsp oil
1 tbsp mustard seeds
1 tbsp cumin seeds
1 green chilli, optional
100g unsweetened desiccated or freshly grated coconut
½ tsp salt
⅛ tsp coconut sugar
2 tbsp lime juice

POTATO CURRY:
1 onion
300g potato
1 green chilli, optional
1 tbsp ground coriander
1 tbsp ground cumin
2 tsp ground turmeric
pinch of salt
pinch of pepper
1 tbsp oil
4 tbsp water

DOSA:
100g FREEE Gram Flour
100g FREEE Rice Flour
¼ tsp salt
350ml water
oil, for frying
lime wedges, to serve

FOR THE COCONUT CHUTNEY:

1   Grate the ginger into a saucepan. Add the oil, mustard seeds and cumin and cook over a gentle heat for 2 minutes. Transfer to a blender.

2   Deseed the chilli, if using, and chop it into the blender. Add the coconut, salt, coconut sugar and lime juice and pulse together. Tip the chutney into a serving dish.

FOR THE POTATO CURRY:

3   Dice the onion and potato into small cubes, then finely dice the chilli, if using.

4   Measure the coriander, cumin, turmeric, salt and pepper into a bowl.

5   Put the oil into a saucepan over a medium heat, add the spices and cook for 1 minute. Add the diced vegetables and cook for 3 minutes, stirring occasionally. Stir in the water and cook gently until the vegetables are tender. Remove the pan from the heat.

FOR THE DOSA:

6   Put the gram flour, rice flour and salt into a large bowl and stir to combine. Add half the water and beat to make a smooth paste. Stir in the remaining water to make a thin batter. Use immediately or cover and chill for up to 12 hours.

7   Lightly oil a frying pan so that the oil just covers the surface and get the pan nice and hot.

8   Stir the batter, then spoon or pour some into the hot pan, rolling it out to the edges to make a 20cm/8 inch wide pancake.

9   Cook the dosa over a medium heat, loosening the edges, until the base is golden. Turn it over and cook the other side. Transfer the dosa onto a plate, cover and keep warm.

10 Repeat until the batter is used.

11 Serve the dosa warm with the spicy potato curry, coconut chutney and fresh lime wedges on the side.

Ring Doughnuts

Whether you call them donuts, or doughnuts, this light and delicious version does have two stages but is surprisingly easy to make. Perfect served warm with a cup of your favourite brew. A ring doughnut baking tray is essential for the first baking stage of making these 6 ring donuts.

MAKES: 6
COOKING TIME: 30 MINUTES

oil, for baking tray and frying
75g FREEE Self Raising
    White Flour
50g FREEE Gram Flour
150g caster sugar
100ml water
1 tsp vanilla extract

1   Preheat the oven to 180°C, Fan 160°C, 350°F, Gas 4. Rub some oil around the inside of a 6-ring doughnut baking tray.

2   Measure the self raising flour, gram flour and 75g of the sugar into a mixing bowl and stir to combine.

3   Add the water and vanilla, stirring to make a smooth batter.

4   Spoon or pipe the batter equally into 6 doughnut rings.

5   Bake for 20 minutes until golden brown. Turn the doughnuts out onto a wire rack.

6   Line a large plate with 2 sheets of kitchen paper. Put the remaining 75g of caster sugar into a bowl.

7   Half-fill a saucepan with oil and put it over a medium heat. Carefully slip a baked doughnut into the hot oil and cook until brown all over, turning over as necessary. Watch and take care as it can brown very quickly if your oil is too hot. Alternatively, you can cook the baked doughnuts in a deep-fat fryer according to the manufacturer's instructions.

8   Using a slotted spoon or tongs, lift the doughnut out of the oil onto the paper-lined plate to drain off any excess oil. Transfer the warm doughnut to the bowl of sugar, then turn it over so it is coated in sugar and leave to cool.

9   Repeat until all doughnuts have been cooked, drained and dredged in sugar.

CHAPTER 5

Pastry, Crumbles & Puddings

Gluten free versions of family
favourites from quiches and
sausage rolls to apple pie, crumbles
and Christmas pudding.

Quiche Lorraine

Quiche Lorraine makes a satisfying meal served both hot and cold. Any leftovers can be wrapped and frozen to enjoy on another day.

SERVES: 4–8
COOKING TIME: 35–40 MINUTES

200g FREEE Plain White
   Flour, plus extra for dusting
½ tsp FREEE Xanthan Gum
pinch of salt
100g butter, plus extra for
   dish or tin
8–9 tbsp cold water

FILLING:
75g bacon cubes
3 eggs
3 tbsp crème fraîche
50g cheese
salt and pepper

1   Measure the flour, xanthan gum and salt into a large bowl and stir to combine.

2   Cube the butter and add to the bowl. Using a fork or pastry blender, work the butter cubes into the flour until the mixture resembles breadcrumbs. Avoid using your fingers for this.

3   Stir in enough of the water to bring the pastry easily together into a soft, slightly sticky ball of dough – it will appear a little wet but will absorb the liquid while resting. Cover the pastry and rest for 15 minutes.

4   Preheat the oven to 180°C, Fan 160°C, 350°F, Gas 4. Rub a little butter around the inside of a 23cm/9 inch round baking dish or tart tin or insert a baking liner.

5   Dust the work surface with flour, put the dough in the middle and sprinkle it with more flour. Roll out the pastry into a circle 5cm/2 inches larger than your dish and lift it in, or press the dough into the dish using your fingers. Cover and chill if not using immediately.

6   Lay a large piece of baking parchment over the raw pastry, making sure all the edges are covered. Scatter the ceramic baking beans (or rice or flour) over the parchment, spreading them all over the surface.

7   Bake for 10–12 minutes. Remove from the oven and carefully lift the baking parchment and contents off the pastry. Return the pastry to the oven and cook for a further 5–6 minutes without browning too much.

FOR THE FILLING:

8   Put the bacon into a frying pan and cook until it changes colour.

9   Meanwhile, put the eggs into a bowl and beat them well, then beat in the crème fraîche. Grate the cheese into the bowl, add the cooked bacon, season with salt and pepper and mix well. Pour the mixture into the pastry case. Bake for 30–35 minutes.

Bakewell Tart

Serve this tart cold with a refreshing cup of afternoon tea, or warm with custard (see page 31) or cream at the end of a meal. Halfway between a pudding and a cake, this traditional English tart has close links with the town of Bakewell in Derbyshire.

g

(see page 31)

SERVES: 8–12
COOKING TIME: 40–45 MINUTES

100g FREEE Plain White Flour, plus extra for dusting
2 tbsp icing sugar
¼ tsp FREEE Xanthan Gum
50g butter, plus extra for tin
1 egg
1–2 tsp cold water

FILLING:
5 tbsp raspberry jam
2 eggs
50g caster sugar
25g FREEE Self Raising White Flour
50g ground almonds
1 tbsp water
25g flaked almonds

1 Preheat the oven to 180°C, Fan 160°C, 350°F, Gas 4. Rub some butter around the inside of a 20cm/8 inch round, loose-bottomed tin.

2 Put the flour, icing sugar and xanthan gum into a bowl, stir to combine, then sift this into a mixing bowl.

3 Cut the butter into small cubes and add them to the bowl. Using a fork or pastry blender, work them together until the mixture resembles breadcrumbs. Avoid using your fingers for this.

4 Add the egg and start to bring together into a pastry dough. Add a teaspoon or two of water if needed to make a slightly sticky dough. Cover the dough and leave it to rest at room temperature for 15 minutes.

5 Dust the work surface with flour, put the pastry in the middle and sprinkle it with more flour. Roll out the pastry into a circle 5cm/2 inches larger than your dish and transfer it to the dish, or simply press it into the baking dish using your fingers. Cut away any pastry that hangs over the edge of your dish and press a fork into the edge of the pastry around the circumference.

FOR THE FILLING:

6 Spoon the jam onto the pastry and spread it out evenly.

7 Put the eggs and caster sugar into a bowl and beat until light and fluffy. Add the flour, ground almonds and water and stir to combine. Spread the mixture over the jam. Sprinkle flaked almonds over the top.

8 Bake for 40–45 minutes.

Pumpkin Pie

Sweet and aromatic, pumpkin pie is a popular autumnal treat when pumpkins and squash are plentiful. You could use the cut-out pieces from making a Halloween jack-o'-lantern (but avoid using any stringy bits) to make this delicious dessert. This recipe is also ideal if you are preparing for a gluten free Thanksgiving.

SERVES: 8–12
COOKING TIME: 30–35 MINUTES

100g FREEE Plain White Flour, plus extra for dusting
1 tbsp icing sugar
¼ tsp FREEE Xanthan Gum
50g butter, plus extra for dish
1 egg
1–2 tbsp orange juice
whipped cream, to serve

PUMPKIN PURÉE:
350g pumpkin or squash
oil, for tray

PUMPKIN PIE FILLING:
75ml evaporated milk
50g sugar
2 tbsp maple syrup
1 egg
2 tsp mixed spice

If you do not have pumpkin or pumpkin purée, then butternut squash will work just as well.

FOR THE PUMPKIN PURÉE:

1. Preheat the oven to 220°C, Fan 200°C, 425°F, Gas 7 if roasting the pumpkin.

2. Chop the pumpkin into small pieces, put the pieces onto a lightly oiled oven tray and bake for 40 minutes until soft. Or put the pumpkin pieces into a pan of water, simmer over a medium heat until soft and drain.

3. When cool enough to handle, remove and discard the pumpkin skin, and put the pulp into a food processor. Pulse the pumpkin into a smooth purée.

FOR THE PASTRY:

4. Reduce the oven temperature to 190°C, Fan 170°C, 375°F, Gas 5. Rub some butter around the inside of a 20cm/8 inch tart or flan dish.

5. Put the flour, icing sugar and xanthan gum into a bowl, stir to combine, then sift into a mixing bowl. Chop the butter into cubes and add them to the bowl. Using a fork or pastry blender, work the butter cubes and flour together until the mixture resembles fine breadcrumbs.

6. Break the egg into the bowl and stir to combine, adding just enough orange juice to make a slightly sticky dough. Cover and leave to rest for 15 minutes.

Continued overleaf →

Pumpkin Pie continued

----

7   Using your hands, gather everything together to form a soft
    ball of pastry dough. Dust the work surface with flour, put the
    pastry in the middle and sprinkle it with more flour. Roll out
    the pastry into a circle 5cm/2 inches larger than your dish and
    lift it into the dish, or simply press the pastry into the dish using
    your fingers. Cut away any pastry that hangs over the edge of
    the dish. Prick the pastry all over with a fork. Lay a large piece
    of baking parchment over the raw pastry, making sure all the
    edges are covered. Scatter the ceramic baking beans (or rice or
    flour) over the baking parchment, spreading them evenly over
    the surface.

8   Bake for 10–12 minutes, remove from the oven and carefully
    lift the baking parchment and contents off the pastry. Return
    the pastry to the oven and cook for a further 4–5 minutes.

    FOR THE FILLING:
9   Put the milk, sugar, maple syrup, egg and mixed spice into a
    bowl and beat together well. Add this to the pumpkin purée
    in the food processor and pulse until smooth. Pour the filling
    into the prepared pastry case.

10 Bake for 30–35 minutes. Delicious served warm or chilled
    with some whipped cream.

Rum and Raisin Celebration Ring

Ideal for a special celebration or as an after-dinner treat, this choux pastry ring is filled with raisins and chestnuts in a lightly boozy cream. The pastry can be made on a baking tray or a ring tin.

SERVES: 8–10
COOKING TIME: 40–45 MINUTES

75g FREEE White Bread Flour
½ tsp caster sugar
2 eggs
50g butter, plus extra for tin
160ml water

FILLING:
50g raisins
50g chestnuts, cooked and
    peeled
2 tbsp rum
150g double cream
25g icing sugar

TOPPING:
50g dark chocolate
50g milk chocolate
75ml double cream
edible gold leaf, optional

1   Preheat the oven to 200°C, Fan 180°C, 400°F, Gas 6. Rub butter generously around the inside of a 23cm/9 inch ring cake tin, or line a large baking tray with a baking liner or baking parchment and draw a 20cm/8 inch circle in the middle as a guide.

2   Sift the flour into a bowl, sprinkle the sugar on top and put it beside the cooker.

3   Break the eggs into another bowl, beat them well and leave this bowl next to the cooker too.

4   Put the butter and water into a saucepan over a medium heat. When the butter has melted and the water has come to the boil, remove the pan from the heat. Immediately add the flour mixture and mix into a thick paste.

5   Return the pan to a gentle heat, stirring vigorously for 30 seconds, to make a soft dough.

6   Remove the pan from the heat again, add a third of the egg and beat it into the dough with a spatula. When it is incorporated, beat in another third of the egg.

7   Beat in the remaining egg to make a thick, smooth paste.

8   Spoon or pipe the warm paste into the ring cake tin, spreading it out evenly, or into a circle using the guide on the prepared baking tray.

9   Bake for 40-45 minutes until golden brown. Remove from the oven, and turn the pastry ring out onto a wire rack. Immediately and carefully, start to cut the pastry in half horizontally, to allow steam to escape. Finish cutting the choux pastry in half and carefully lift off the top half. Leave to cool.

Continued overleaf →

Rum and Raisin Celebration Ring continued

FOR THE FILLING:

10 Measure the raisins into a bowl. Quarter the chestnuts and
    add these to the bowl. Pour over the rum, stir, cover and leave
    to soak overnight.

11 Pour the cream into a large mixing bowl and beat until thick.
    Sift the icing sugar over the cream and stir to combine. Add
    the soaked raisins and chestnuts and stir gently to combine.
    Spoon the filling into the choux pastry base. Replace the top
    half of the choux pastry over the base.

FOR THE TOPPING:

12 Break both types of chocolate into small pieces.

13 Measure the cream into a saucepan and put it over a gentle
    heat. As soon as small bubbles appear in the cream, remove
    the pan from the heat. Add the chocolate pieces, shake the pan
    and stand for a minute. Stir gently until smooth. Drizzle the
    chocolate topping over the top of the choux pastry and leave
    to set.

14 Sprinkle a little edible gold leaf over the top and chill until
    ready to serve.

Jam Tarts

You can use almost any type of jam to make these 12 classic, individual tarts. If you don't eat them all at once, wrap and freeze them for another day.

MAKES: 12
COOKING TIME: 20–25 MINUTES

100g FREEE Plain White Flour, plus extra for dusting
1 tsp icing sugar
¼ tsp FREEE Xanthan Gum
50g butter, plus extra for tray
1 egg
1–2 tsp water
4 tbsp jam of your choice

1   Preheat the oven to 190°C, Fan 170°C, 375°F, Gas 5. Rub some butter around the inside of a 12-hole tart tray.

2   Put the flour, icing sugar and xanthan gum into a bowl, stir to combine, then sift this into a mixing bowl.

3   Cut the butter into small cubes and add them to the bowl. Using a fork or pastry blender, work them together until the mixture resembles fine breadcrumbs.

4   Add the egg and start to bring together into a pastry dough.

5   Add a teaspoon or two of water, if needed, to make a slightly sticky dough. Cover and leave the dough to rest for 15 minutes.

6   Dust the work surface with flour, put the pastry in the middle and sprinkle it with more flour. Roll out the dough until 3mm/⅛ inch thick. Using a round pastry cutter or cup slightly larger than the tart holes, cut out 12 pastry circles. Transfer the dough circles to the prepared tart tray.

7   Put a teaspoon of jam into each tart, taking care not to overfill them or the jam will overflow during cooking.

8   Bake for 20–25 minutes.

Star Mince Tarts

These delightful mincemeat pies look very attractive and are a little lighter to eat than those with a full pastry lid. Use the best mincemeat you can find or perhaps make your own using dried fruit, butter, grated apple and a little syrup.

OPTION:

MAKES: 12
COOKING TIME: 25 MINUTES

200g FREEE Plain White
    Flour, plus extra for dusting
25g icing sugar
½ tsp FREEE Xanthan Gum
100g butter or plant butter
1 egg
1–2 tbsp cold water

FILLING AND TOPPING:
200g gluten free mincemeat
1 tbsp apricot jam, warmed

1   Measure the flour, icing sugar and xanthan gum into a bowl, stir to combine, then sift into a mixing bowl.

2   Cut the butter into small cubes and add them to the bowl.

3   Using a fork or pastry blender, work the butter into the flour until the mixture resembles breadcrumbs. Avoid using your fingers for this.

4   Break the egg into the bowl and stir in enough of the water to bring the pastry easily together into a soft, slightly sticky ball of dough. Cover and rest the pastry for 15 minutes.

5   Preheat the oven to 180°C, Fan 160°C, 350°F, Gas 4. Rub some butter around the insides of a 12-hole tart tray.

6   Cut off a third of the dough and leave it to continue resting. Dust the work surface with flour, put the larger piece of dough in the middle and sprinkle it with flour. Roll out the pastry until it is 3mm/⅛ inch thick. Select a pastry cutter or cup a little bigger than the holes of the tart tray and press it into the dough to make circles. Lift the circles onto the prepared tray.

FOR THE FILLING AND TOPPING:
7   Put 1 teaspoon of mincemeat in the centre of each tart.

8   Roll out the remaining pastry on the floured surface and press a small star cutter into the dough to make star shapes. Gently place these over the mincemeat.

9   Bake for 25 minutes. Remove the tart tray from the oven, brush the pastry stars with a little apricot jam and cook for a further 5 minutes.

Treacle Tart

A classic treacle tart, made with rice flour sweet pastry, gluten free breadcrumbs, golden syrup and a hint of lemon.

SERVES: 8–12
COOKING TIME: 40–48 MINUTES

100g FREEE Rice Flour,
   plus extra for dusting
1 tbsp icing sugar
¼ tsp FREEE Xanthan Gum
50g butter, plus extra for
   tin or dish
1 egg
1–2 tsp lemon juice

FILLING:
1 egg
1 tsp finely grated lemon rind
350g golden syrup
50g gluten free breadcrumbs

1 Preheat the oven to 190°C, Fan 170°C, 375°F, Gas 5. Rub some butter around the inside of a 20cm/8 inch loose-bottomed tart tin or flan dish.

2 Measure the flour, icing sugar and xanthan gum into a bowl, stir to combine, then sift into a mixing bowl.

3 Cut the butter into small cubes and add them to the mixing bowl. Using a fork, work the butter into the flour until the mixture resembles fine breadcrumbs. Avoid using your fingers for this.

4 Break the egg into the bowl and stir to combine, adding just enough lemon juice to make a slightly sticky dough.

5 Using your hands, gather everything together to form a smooth ball of pastry dough. Cover and leave to rest for 15 minutes.

6 Dust the work surface with flour, put the dough in the middle and sprinkle it with more flour. Roll out the pastry into a circle 5cm/2 inches larger than your dish and lift it into the dish, or simply press the dough into the dish using your fingers. Lay a large piece of baking parchment over the raw pastry, making sure all the edges are covered. Scatter the ceramic baking beans (or rice or flour) over the baking parchment, spreading them evenly over the surface.

7 Bake for 15–18 minutes, then remove from the oven and carefully lift the parchment and contents off the pastry. Return the pastry to the oven and cook for a further 5–6 minutes.

FOR THE FILLING:
8 Break the egg into a mixing bowl, add the lemon rind to the bowl and whisk together well. Continue whisking as you add the golden syrup.

9 Add the breadcrumbs, stir until combined, then let the mixture stand for 5 minutes.

10 Tip the mixture into the pastry case and bake for 25–30 minutes.

Lemon Tart

Serve this delicious lemon tart as a summer dessert on its own or with a few summer berries. It can be made in advance and frozen, then simply defrosted for 1 hour before serving. Cover and refrigerate the spare egg whites to make meringues (see page 172) or gluten free bread (see pages 114–122) on another occasion.

SERVES: 8–12
COOKING TIME: 42–52 MINUTES

100g FREEE Plain White Flour, plus extra for dusting
25g icing sugar, plus extra to serve
pinch of FREEE Xanthan Gum
50g butter, plus extra for dish
3 eggs
1 tsp water, optional
redcurrants, to serve (optional)

FILLING:
2 eggs
100g caster sugar
100ml lemon juice
150g double cream

1   Preheat the oven to 190°C, Fan 170°C, 375°F, Gas 5. Rub some butter around the inside of 20cm/8 inch tart or flan dish or insert a baking liner.

2   Measure the flour, icing sugar and xanthan gum into a bowl, stir to combine and sift into a mixing bowl.

3   Cut the butter into small cubes and add them to the bowl. Using a fork or pastry blender, work them together until the mixture resembles fine breadcrumbs.

4   Separate the egg yolks and whites into separate bowls. Cover and save the egg whites for another occasion.

5   Add the egg yolks to the mixing bowl and stir to combine. If it does not do this easily, add 1 teaspoon of water.

6   Using your hands, gather everything together to form a ball of pastry dough. Cover and rest for 15 minutes.

7   Dust the work surface with flour, put the pastry in the middle and sprinkle it with flour. Roll out the pastry into a circle 5cm/2 inches larger than your dish and transfer it to the dish, or simply press the dough into the dish using your fingers. Cut away any pastry that hangs over the edge of the dish. Prick the pastry all over with a fork. Lay a large piece of baking parchment over the raw pastry, making sure all the edges are covered. Scatter ceramic baking beans (or rice or flour) over the baking parchment, spreading them all over the surface.

Continued overleaf →

----

8   Bake for 12–15 minutes. Remove from the oven and carefully lift the baking parchment and contents off the pastry. Return the pastry to the oven and cook for a further 10–12 minutes without browning too much. Take the dish out of the oven and leave to cool.

FOR THE FILLING:

9   Reduce the oven temperature to 150°C, Fan 130°C, 300°F, Gas 2.

10 Break the eggs into a mixing bowl and whisk well. Add the sugar and whisk until the mixture thickens slightly. Whisk in the lemon juice. Stir in the cream. Pour the mixture into the pastry case.

11 Bake for 20–25 minutes – the filling should be just wobbly. Turn off the oven, leaving the tart inside for 10 minutes. Remove from the oven and leave to cool completely.

12 When cool, chill the tart until required.

13 Serve the tart with a few redcurrants (optional) and/or dusted with a little icing sugar.

Baked Cheesecake

Surprisingly less rich than chilled cheesecakes, this flavoursome baked cheesecake is lovely to serve with a hot drink and equally delicious with a little cream as a dessert.

SERVES: 8–12
COOKING TIME: 70 MINUTES

250g ricotta
4 eggs
150g caster sugar
2 tsp finely grated orange rind
500g mascarpone
75g FREEE Plain White Flour
50g sultanas

1   Preheat the oven to 170°C, Fan 150°C, 300°F, Gas 2. Line a 18cm/7 inch deep round baking tin with baking parchment.

2   Put the ricotta into a sieve over a bowl to drain away the liquid.

3   Separate the eggs, putting the yolks in one mixing bowl and the whites into another. Add the sugar to the yolks and beat until they are slightly thickened.

4   Add the orange rind to the bowl. Press the ricotta to drain off any extra liquid then add it to the bowl with the mascarpone and mix everything together until smooth.

5   Beat the egg whites until stiff. Using a metal spoon, gently fold the egg whites into the mixing bowl until roughly combined.

6   Sift the flour into the bowl, add the sultanas and gently fold everything together.

7   Tip the mixture into the prepared tin and smooth the top.

8   Bake for 70 minutes. Turn the oven off without opening the door. Leave the cheesecake in the oven until it is cool, about 3–4 hours.

9   Remove the cheesecake, which may have sunk a little in the middle, from the oven. Turn out onto a plate and chill until ready to serve.

Lemon Zest Cheesecake

This fresh and lemony cheesecake is very easy to make and requires no baking. The base is made from crushed Lemon Zest Cookies, although you could swap these for Ginger Cookies.

SERVES: 8–12

150g FREEE Lemon Zest
   Cookies
50g butter, plus extra for
   dish or tin
400g full-fat cream cheese
75g icing sugar
2 tsp finely grated lemon rind
3 tbsp lemon juice
lemon slices, to decorate

1 Rub some butter around the inside of a 18cm/7 inch round dish or loose-bottomed tin.

2 Put the cookies into a bag, crush them into fine crumbs and tip them into a mixing bowl.

3 Melt the butter and stir it into the crushed biscuit crumbs. Press the mixture into the prepared dish and leave to chill for 1 hour.

4 Tip the cream cheese into a mixing bowl, sift in the icing sugar and mix them together. Add the lemon rind and juice to the bowl and stir to combine. Scoop the mixture onto the crumb base and smooth the top.

5 Chill the cheesecake until the top is set.

6 Decorate with very small pieces of sliced lemon.

Strawberry Tart

This delightful tart has a sweet rice flour pastry base with a crème pâtissière filling and is topped with fresh strawberries. You could also use raspberries, blackberries and redcurrants.

SERVES: 8–12
COOKING TIME: 25–30 MINUTES

100g FREEE Rice Flour,
    plus extra for dusting
1 tbsp icing sugar
¼ tsp FREEE Xanthan Gum
50g butter, plus extra for tin
    or dish
1 egg
1–2 tbsp orange juice

CRÈME PÂTISSIÈRE:
3 tbsp icing sugar
1 tbsp FREEE Cornflour
2 egg yolks
2 tbsp water
150ml milk

TOPPING:
250g strawberries
1 tbsp redcurrant jelly

1 Preheat the oven to 190°C, Fan 170°C, 375°F, Gas 5. Rub some butter around the inside of a 20cm/8 inch loose-bottomed tart tin or flan dish.

2 Put the flour, icing sugar and xanthan gum into a bowl, stir to combine, then sift into a mixing bowl.

3 Cut the butter into small cubes and add them to the mixing bowl. Using a fork or pastry blender, work them together until the mixture resembles fine breadcrumbs. Avoid using your fingers for this. Break the egg into the bowl and stir to combine, adding just enough orange juice to make a slightly sticky dough.

4 Using your hands, gather everything together to form a smooth ball of pastry dough. Cover and leave to rest for 15 minutes.

5 Dust the work surface with flour, put the dough in the middle and sprinkle it with more flour. Roll out the pastry into a circle 5cm/2 inches larger than your dish and lift it into the dish, or simply press the dough into the dish using your fingers.

6 Lay a large piece of baking parchment over the raw pastry, making sure all the edges are covered. Scatter the ceramic baking beans (or rice or flour) over the baking parchment, spreading them evenly over the surface.

7 Bake for 15–18 minutes, then remove from the oven and carefully lift the baking parchment and contents off the pastry. Return the pastry to the oven and cook for a further 10–12 minutes until the pastry just starts to turn golden. Leave to cool.

FOR THE CRÈME PÂTISSIÈRE:

8 Put the sugar, cornflour, egg yolks and water into a large bowl and mix to a smooth paste.

9 Heat the milk in a saucepan until it comes to the boil. Pour the milk into the bowl and stir well, then pour everything

back into the saucepan. Gently bring back to the boil, stirring continuously, until thick and smooth. Allow to bubble for a few moments while still stirring, then remove from the heat.

10 Pour the crème pâtissière into the cooked pastry case and leave to cool completely.

FOR THE TOPPING:

11 Arrange the strawberries on the cold crème pâtissière.

12 Gently warm the redcurrant jelly. Brush the jelly over the strawberries. Chill the tart until ready to serve.

Sticky Toffee Pudding

An all-time family favourite, with a rich treacle flavour. This pudding, which can be made in 6 ramekins or a large dish, may sink a little in the middle but will still taste fantastic! It is delicious served with cream, vanilla ice cream or custard (see page 31).

(see page 31)

MAKES: 6 SMALL OR 1 LARGE
COOKING TIME: 20–30 MINUTES,
DEPENDING ON SIZE

75g stoned dates
100ml boiling water
½ tsp FREEE Bicarbonate
 of Soda
75g butter, plus extra for
 ramekins or baking dish
75g brown sugar
1 egg
1 tbsp black treacle
75g FREEE Self Raising
 White Flour

1 Chop the dates into a bowl and add the boiling water. Stir in the bicarbonate of soda then set aside to cool.

2 Preheat the oven to 200°C, Fan 180°C, 400°F, Gas 6. Rub a little butter around the inside of 6 ramekins or a 1.1 litre/2 pint baking dish.

3 Cut the butter into small cubes and put them into a mixing bowl. Add the sugar and beat together until softened.

4 Break the egg into the bowl, add the treacle and beat well.

5 Sift the flour into the bowl and stir to combine.

6 Mash the cold date mixture into a purée, add it to the mixing bowl and beat well.

7 Divide the mixture between the ramekin dishes or the baking dish and smooth the top.

8 Bake for 20–30 minutes, depending on size, and until a cocktail stick comes out clean. Don't worry if the pudding sinks slightly in the middle.

9 Leave to cool for a few minutes, then turn out the pudding(s) onto a plate(s). Alternatively, leave to cool completely, then gently reheat and turn out when warmed through.

Plum Crumble

Make the most of the plum season with this comforting gluten free plum crumble recipe. Cream, yoghurt, custard (see page 31) or plant-based alternatives are an ideal accompaniment to crumble.

OPTION:

SERVES: 8–12
COOKING TIME: 35–40 MINUTES

600g plums
175g caster sugar
3 tbsp water
250g FREEE Plain White Flour
25g demerara sugar
150g butter or plant butter
1 tbsp FREEE Porridge Oats

1   Preheat the oven to 180°C, Fan 160°C, 350°F, Gas 4.

2   Wash the plums and put them into a 1.1 litre/2 pint oven dish, or wash and slice the plums, remove the stones and put them into your dish. Add 50g of the caster sugar and water and stir to mix.

3   Measure the flour, remaining 125g caster sugar and the demerara sugar into a mixing bowl. Slice the butter into lumps, add these to the bowl and roughly mix with a fork, to create lumpy breadcrumbs.

4   Tip the mixture over the fruit and level the top. Sprinkle the oats over the top.

5   Bake for 35–40 minutes.

Oat Apple Crumble

Made with eating apples for natural sweetness this vegan, sugar free crumble has a crunchy granola-style topping and is also naturally gluten free. We made one large crumble but you could make several smaller ones and freeze any you don't eat to enjoy another day.

SERVES: 8–12
COOKING TIME: 55–60 MINUTES

150g FREEE Porridge Oats
50g flaked almonds
50g pumpkin seeds
4 tbsp maple syrup
4 tbsp oil
1 tsp vanilla extract
6 eating apples
150ml water

1   Preheat the oven to 180°C, Fan 160°C, 350°F, Gas 4.

2   Put the oats, flaked almonds and pumpkin seeds into a mixing bowl. Add the maple syrup, oil and vanilla and mix together thoroughly.

3   Peel, core and roughly chop the apples into a 1.1 litre/2 pint oven dish. Pour the water over the apples. Tip the prepared oat mixture over the apples, spreading it out to the edges.

4   Bake for 55–60 minutes, less if making smaller crumbles.

Christmas Pudding

The best way to finish your Christmas lunch is with a traditional Christmas pudding. Your pudding needs to be pre-cooked either by simmering it in a saucepan or cooking in a microwave, and it is then reheated before serving. For a grand finale to a special lunch, you could flame the Christmas pudding before serving.

SERVES: 8–12
COOKING TIME: 2 HOURS OR 7 MINUTES, DEPENDING ON COOKING METHOD

100g FREEE White Bread Flour
100g soft brown sugar
2 tsp mixed spice
50g prunes
50g dried apricots
125g raisins
125g sultanas
175g currants
50g mixed peel
rind and juice of 1 orange
rind and juice of 1 lemon
50g oil, plus extra for pudding basin

DECORATION, OPTIONAL:
bay leaves or rosemary
redcurrants or cranberries
3–4 tbsp brandy or rum

The pudding keeps well and is usually made well ahead of the seasonal festivities (1–3 months in advance) to allow the flavours to fully mature.

1 Measure the flour, sugar and mixed spice into a bowl and stir to combine.

2 Chop the prunes and apricots into a large mixing bowl, add the raisins, sultanas, currants and mixed peel. Add the orange and lemon rinds and juice. Stir in the oil.

3 Stir the prepared flour into the bowl and mix well. Cover and leave the mixture to stand for at least 2 hours or overnight.

4 Cut 2 circles of baking parchment to fit just inside the top of a 1.1 litre/2 pint pudding basin. Rub some oil around the inside of the pudding basin.

5 Stir the mixture, tip it into the pudding basin, pushing it down and smoothing the top. Cover the top of the pudding with the prepared parchment circles.

COOKING THE PUDDING IN A SAUCEPAN:

6 Cover the pudding basin with kitchen foil, tucking it in well around the outer rim.

7 Stand the pudding in the bottom of a large pan and add boiling water until it comes halfway up the pudding basin. Put the lid on the saucepan and simmer gently for 2 hours. Lift the lid occasionally and add more boiling water to keep the level halfway up the pudding basin.

8 Once cooked, leave the pudding to cool without removing the kitchen foil and baking parchment. Store the pudding in a cool, dark place for 1–3 months and reheat to serve.

Continued overleaf →

6 Cover the pudding with clingfilm and cut a hole in the top for steam to escape.

7 Cook on medium high (600W) for 3 minutes, leave to stand for 1 minute and cook for a further 3 minutes. Leave the pudding to cool completely.

8 Remove the clingfilm and cover the basin tightly with kitchen foil. Store the pudding in a cool, dark place for 1–3 months and reheat to serve.

Reheating in a Microwave, on the Hob or in the Oven

MICROWAVE:

1 Remove the kitchen foil, check the pudding is in good condition and replace the parchment layer. Re-cover the pudding loosely with clingfilm, which will allow steam to escape.

2 Put the pudding into the microwave and close the door. Turn the microwave to full power (800W). Cook the pudding for 3 minutes, then leave to stand for 2 minutes.

3 Carefully remove the pudding dish from the microwave. Remove the clingfilm and baking parchment. Run a warm knife around the inside edge of the bowl. Put a warm plate on top of the pudding basin, carefully invert the pudding and let it slide onto the plate.

4 Keep warm until serving. Decorate with a bay leaf or sprig of rosemary and a few cranberries or redcurrants before serving.

HOB:

1 Remove the kitchen foil, check the pudding is in good condition and replace the parchment layer. Re-cover the pudding dish with kitchen foil, tucking it in well at the outer rim.

2 Stand the pudding in the bottom of a large pan and add boiling water until it comes halfway up the pudding dish. Set the hob control for gentle simmering. Put the lid on the pan and simmer gently for 1 hour. Check the hot water halfway and refill if needed.

3 Carefully remove the pudding dish from the saucepan of hot water. Remove the kitchen foil and baking parchment. Run a warm knife around the inside edge of the bowl. Put a warm plate on top of the pudding basin, carefully invert the pudding and let it slide onto the plate.

4 Keep warm until serving. Decorate with a bay leaf or sprig of rosemary and a few cranberries or redcurrants before serving.

OVEN:

1 Remove the kitchen foil, check the pudding is in good condition and replace the parchment layer. Re-cover the pudding dish with kitchen foil, tucking it in well at the outer rim.

2 Stand the pudding in the bottom of a deep oven dish and add boiling water until it comes halfway up the pudding dish. Preheat the oven to 180°C, Fan 160°C, 350°F, Gas 4.

3 Cover the oven dish with a lid or kitchen foil and bake in the hot oven for 30 minutes. Check and refill the hot water halfway if needed.

4 Carefully remove the pudding dish from the dish of hot water. Remove the kitchen foil and baking parchment. Run a warm knife around the inside edge of the bowl. Put a warm plate on top of the pudding basin, carefully invert the pudding and let it slide onto the plate.

5 Keep warm until serving. Decorate with a bay leaf or sprig of rosemary and a few cranberries or redcurrants before serving.

HOW TO FLAME A CHRISTMAS PUDDING:

1. If flaming the pudding, remove the bay leaf and decoration. Put 3–4 tablespoons of brandy or rum into a small saucepan and warm gently without letting it boil. Remove the pan from the heat and pour the hot alcohol over the plated pudding.

2. Carefully ignite the alcohol with a lighter straight away. Before the flame subsides, tilt the serving plate and spoon any liquid back over the pudding. The flame will disappear when all the alcohol has burnt away.

3. Allow the flames to subside before serving.

CHAPTER 6

Pizza, Dumplings & Pasta

Make gluten free versions of some of the most loved foods for mealtimes, from pizza, pasta and dumplings to stuffing balls, gnocchi and onion bhajis.

Thin and Crispy Tomato and Goat's Cheese Pizza

This tasty, light and crunchy pizza has a yeast-free base. Serve warm slices of this 23cm/9 inch pizza with a green salad or cut into fun-sized pieces for snacking.

MAKES: 1
COOKING TIME: 15 MINUTES
PLUS 15–20 MINUTES

150g FREEE White Bread Flour
2 tsp FREEE Baking Powder
½ tsp salt
150ml milk
4 tbsp olive oil, plus extra for baking tray

TOPPING:
250g tomatoes
125g goat's cheese, sliced
½ tsp dried basil
fresh basil leaves
salt and pepper

1 Twenty minutes before you are going to bake, preheat the oven to 220°C, Fan 200°C, 425°F, Gas 7.

2 Rub some oil around the inside of a large baking tray or insert a baking liner.

3 Measure the flour, baking powder and salt into a bowl, stir to combine, then sift into a mixing bowl.

4 Add the milk and 3 tablespoons of the olive oil and stir into a smooth thick paste.

5 Sprinkle the remaining spoon of oil over the paste and using a spatula, scrape the paste into a doughy mass.

6 Tip the doughy mass onto the baking tray and using the spatula, spread and press the doughy mass into a 30cm/ 12 inch circle.

7 Bake for 15 minutes. Remove from the oven.

FOR THE TOPPING:
8 Slice the tomatoes thinly and lay these over the pizza base. Lay the goat's cheese over the tomatoes. Sprinkle the dried basil over the top. Season well with salt and pepper.

9 Bake for 15–20 minutes.

10 Slice and serve warm, topped with fresh basil leaves.

Homemade Pasta

You can make your own gluten free tagliatelle or lasagne with a few simple ingredients and a pasta machine. Use the flat sheets to make a lasagne or cut them into tagliatelle and enjoy with your favourite pasta sauce.

SERVES: 2
COOKING TIME: 3–8 MINUTES

75g FREEE White Bread Flour, plus extra for dusting
pinch of salt
¼ tsp FREEE Xanthan Gum
1 egg

TO COOK:
1 litre boiling water
pinch of fine salt
olive oil, for sprinkling

1   Put the flour, salt and xanthan gum into a mixing bowl and stir to combine. Sift into another mixing bowl. Make a depression in the middle of the flour. Break the egg into the middle and beat together, allowing a little flour to be incorporated each time you stir. Continue stirring as the flour mixes in, eventually forming a dough. Cover and chill the dough for 30 minutes.

2   Cut the dough into 4 pieces and roll each into a smooth ball. Dust the pasta machine and the table liberally with flour. Flatten each piece of dough and pass it through the widest, flat roller of a pasta machine to make a rectangle.

3   Fold the dough in half and pass it though the roller twice more.

4   Decrease the roller width a couple of notches and pass each rectangle through a couple of times to help it hold together. If the dough seems sticky, dust with flour. Continue reducing the roller width, rolling each rectangle thinner until it is 1mm thick.

5   Use the pasta sheets in a lasagne or pass them through the tagliatelle cutter.

6   Lay the tagliatelle out or hang it over the edge of a tall saucepan to dry for 1 hour. Uncooked pasta can be chilled for up to 24 hours before using.

TO COOK TAGLIATELLE:
7   Put the water and salt into a large saucepan and bring it to a rolling boil. Add the pasta and stir to ensure it is free flowing. Cook for 3–8 minutes, depending on the size and thickness of the pasta.

8   Drain the pasta and sprinkle with a little olive oil.

Gnocchi with Tomato Sauce

Simple ingredients are transformed into these bite-sized dumplings to make a lovely lunch or supper dish for 2–3 people. Both the gnocchi and the tomato sauce can be prepared in advance, with the final cooking minutes before you want to eat. You can use fresh or tinned tomatoes for the tomato sauce. Uncooked gluten free gnocchi freeze well and can be cooked from frozen.

SERVES: 2–3
COOKING TIME: 7–14 MINUTES
FOR THE GNOCCHI

300g potato
1 egg
¼ tsp salt
⅛ tsp pepper
pinch of nutmeg
25g Parmesan, plus extra
   to serve
75g FREEE White Bread Flour,
   plus extra for dusting
1 tbsp olive oil

TOMATO SAUCE:
3 tbsp olive oil
1 onion, finely chopped
2 garlic cloves, finely diced
400g tomatoes, chopped
1 tbsp tomato purée
½ tsp mixed herbs
¼ tsp salt
⅛ tsp pepper
pinch of brown sugar

1. Put the unpeeled potato and some water into a saucepan over a medium heat and cook until soft and cooked. Drain the potato, peel and discard the potato skin.

2. Press the potato through a ricer into a mixing bowl or mash well with a fork.

3. Break the egg into the bowl, add the salt, pepper and nutmeg and mix thoroughly.

4. Finely grate the Parmesan into the bowl and stir to combine.

5. Add the flour and mix everything together.

6. Using your hands, gather everything together into a smooth ball of dough.

7. Lightly dust a chopping board with flour, put the dough in the middle and dust it with more flour if it is sticky. Cut the dough into three pieces and roll each one into a 23cm/9 inch cylinder.

8. Cut each cylinder into quarters and then each piece of dough into 3 pieces. Gently press the tines of a fork onto each piece of dough to make lines. Chill until required.

Continued overleaf →

Gnocchi with Tomato Sauce continued

- -

FOR THE TOMATO SAUCE:

9   Measure the oil into a saucepan, add the onion and garlic, cover and cook over a gentle heat for 3–5 minutes until soft. Add the tomatoes to the pan with the tomato purée. Stir, cover and simmer gently for 5–6 minutes. Add the mixed herbs, salt and pepper and pinch of brown sugar and stir to combine.

10 Remove from the heat and use a stick blender to roughly purée the sauce.

11 Bring a large pan of lightly salted water to a rolling boil. Add the gnocchi and simmer for 2–4 minutes until they rise to the surface. Drain the gnocchi, return them to the pan and sprinkle over the oil.

12 Serve the warm gnocchi with warm tomato sauce and a sprinkling of Parmesan.

Herb Dumplings

Dumplings, made with or without herbs, are a quick, easy and hearty addition to soups, stews and casseroles. This recipe makes 8 dumplings. Simply add the dumplings 20–25 minutes before the end of the cooking time. It's always wise to check the ingredients on your suet label are suitable for your dietary needs.

MAKES: 8
COOKING TIME: 20–25 MINUTES

150g FREEE Plain White Flour
3 tsp FREEE Baking Powder
¼ tsp salt
¼ tsp pepper
75g gluten free vegetable suet
2 tsp mixed dried herbs
125ml cold water
1 litre soup or gluten free stock

1   Measure the flour, baking powder, salt and pepper into a bowl, stir to combine, then sift into a mixing bowl.

2   Stir in the suet and herbs. Add the water and stir to make a slightly soft and sticky dough. Cover and leave to stand for 30 minutes.

3   Divide the dough into 8 pieces and lightly roll each piece into a ball.

4   Bring the soup or stock to the boil and gently add the dumplings. Continue to boil gently for 20–25 minutes.

Sage and Onion Stuffing Balls

Everyone loves stuffing balls; however, you might prefer to stuff a bird, or for ease bake your stuffing in an oiled oven tray. The recipe makes 12 stuffing balls. These stuffing balls are made with gluten free breadcrumbs which can be made in advance, then bagged and frozen for using when you make your stuffing.

MAKES: 12
COOKING TIME: 30–35 MINUTES

150g gluten free, dairy free
  bread
75g small onion, finely diced
100ml boiling water
1 tbsp oil, plus extra for
  baking tray
1 tbsp sage, chopped
1 egg
salt and pepper

TO MAKE THE BREADCRUMBS:

1   Remove the crusts from the bread and discard, cut the crumb into slices and then into chunks. Using your fingers, break the chunks into smaller chunks and spread them out on a baking tray. Cover loosely with a clean tea towel and leave overnight to become stale.

2   Transfer to a food processor and pulse lightly to make breadcrumbs. If not using immediately, the breadcrumbs can be bagged and frozen for up to a month.

TO MAKE THE STUFFING BALLS:

3   Bring the breadcrumbs up to room temperature.

4   Put the onion into a mixing bowl, pour over the boiling water and leave to stand for 15 minutes.

5   Preheat the oven to 200°C, Fan 180°C, 400°F, Gas 6. Rub some oil around the inside of a baking tray.

6   Drain the water from the onion, add it to the mixing bowl and stir to combine. Add the oil, sage, egg, salt and pepper and mix together well. If not using immediately, the stuffing can be bagged and frozen for up to a month.

7   Divide the mixture into 12 mounds and roll each into a ball. Transfer the stuffing balls to the prepared tray.

8   Bake for 30–35 minutes. Cooked stuffing balls can be frozen and reheated from frozen.

Onion Bhajis

These well-known savoury snacks are delicious served warm with plain yoghurt and chutney, stuffed into pitta bread or to accompany curry dishes. This recipe makes 10 bhajis.

MAKES: 10
COOKING TIME: 3–4 MINUTES
PER BHAJI

75g FREEE Gram Flour
2 tsp cumin seeds
1 tsp ground coriander
1 tsp ground turmeric
½ tsp salt
½ tsp mixed spice
4 tbsp water
50g potato
100g onion
5 tbsp oil

1   Line an oven dish with 2 sheets of kitchen paper.

2   Put the gram flour, cumin seeds, coriander, turmeric, salt, mixed spice and water into a mixing bowl and stir to make a paste.

3   Finely grate the potato and coarsely grate the onion. Tip them into the mixing bowl and stir thoroughly.

4   Put the oil into a frying pan over a medium heat. Take a rounded spoon of the mixture and carefully slide it into the hot pan. Cook the bhaji, turning it regularly, until golden brown on all sides, or cook bhajis in a deep-fat fryer according to the manufacturer's instructions.

5   Using a slotted spoon, lift the bhaji onto the prepared oven dish and cover to keep warm.

6   Repeat the cooking process with the remaining bhaji mixture.

Index

Conversion tables

Cake Tin Size Conversion Table

If you don't have the exact size of cake tin specified in a recipe, you may be able to use another in your cupboard. This reference table offers some square and rectangular tin options which should be the same depth as the tin you want to replace.

Round Tin	Square Tin	Rectangular Tin
10cm/4inches	7.5cm/3 x 3 inches	-
15cm/6 inches	12.5 x 12.5cm/5 x 5 inches	10 x 15cm/4 x 6 inches
18cm/7 inches	15 x 15cm/6 x 6 inches	12.5 x 18cm/5 x 7 inches
20cm/8 inches	18 x 18cm/7 x 7 inches	15 x 20cm/6 x 8 inches
23cm/9 inches	20 x 20cm/8 x 8 inches	18 x 23cm/7 x 9 inches
25cm/10 inches	23 x 23cm/9 x 9 inches	18 x 30cm/7 x 12 inches
28cm/11 inches	25 x 25cm/10 x 10 inches	23 x 28cm/9 x 11 inches
30cm/12 inches	28 x 28cm/11 x 11 inches	25 x 30cm/10 x 12 inches
35cm/14 inches	30 x 30cm/12 x 12 inches	28 x 33cm/11 x 13 inches

Oven Temperatures Conversion Table

Gas	°F	°C	Fan °C
1	275	140	120
2	300	150	130
3	325	170	150
4	350	180	160
5	375	190	170
6	400	200	180
7	425	220	200
8	450	230	210
9	475	240	220

Imperial to Metric Conversion Table

Ounces	Grams
½oz	10g
¾oz	20g
1oz	25g
1½oz	40g
2oz	50g
2½oz	60g
3oz	75g
4oz	110g
4½oz	125g
5oz	150g
6oz	175g
7oz	200g
8oz	225g
9oz	250g
10oz	275g
12oz	350g
1lb	450g
1lb 8oz	700g
2lb	900g
3lb	1.35kg

Thank you

To my husband Michael, children Jethro, Rupert and Madeleine, who have all eaten their way through the years of test baking that created the recipes in this book. We have had fun talking about food, baking and eating together, and I have appreciated their critique as well as many smiling, contented faces. To my Mother, mentioned several times in this book, who always encouraged me to experiment with ingredients and enjoy eating.

To Thomas Barkholt for curating and co-ordinating the many aspects of FREEE baking, to Rachel Elmore for her patient proofreading and to test baker Eva Gyorfi.

To my publisher, Elizabeth Bond at Ebury for helping conceive the book and steering me through the process with a firm hand. Thank you to all the editorial and creative teams who work behind the scenes especially Izzy Frost, Liz & Max Haarala Hamilton, Bella Haycraft Mee and Sassy Stewart-Wilson.

To the entire FREEE team at Doves Farm Foods, who work tirelessly every day to produce delicious and safe gluten free flours and other foods, which help thousands of people enjoy gluten free baking.

And finally, a big thank you to all the people who over the years have tried my bakes, and given me invaluable feedback to keep improving, evolving and perfecting this collection of some of my favourite gluten free recipes.

About the author

Clare Marriage is the CEO and managing director of Wiltshire-based, family-owned company Doves Farm Foods Ltd, which she founded with her husband Michael in the seventies. The business is considered pioneering in artisan, free from and organic foods.

Inspired to cook and bake from an early age by her mother's fondness for cooking fresh, seasonal food, Clare was destined for a career in food. While still at university, she set up and ran her own catering company specialising in wholegrain based meals, before starting Doves Farm Foods after she met Michael, who had a background in milling and farming.

Around the same time, her mother was advised to follow a gluten free diet and this started her journey into gluten free foods in earnest. A desire to help anyone gluten free to bake delicious sweet and savoury dishes using speciality ingredients led to the creation of the FREEE flours and a broader gluten free product range. Four decades on, Clare was awarded a Free From Hero Award in 2017 in recognition of her contribution to the development of the gluten free food movement in the UK.

Surprisingly perhaps, this is Clare's first book, but as a passionate cook and baker, Clare has been creating and sharing recipes with the world for many years on www.dovesfarm.co.uk and www.freee-foods.co.uk. Her recipes are also frequently featured in the press.

1

Ebury Press, an imprint of Ebury Publishing
20 Vauxhall Bridge Road
London SW1V 2SA

Ebury Press is part of the Penguin Random House group of companies
whose addresses can be found at global.penguinrandomhouse.com

Photography: Haarala Hamilton
Design: Louise Evans
Food Stylist: Bella Haycraft Mee
Prop Stylist: Rachel Vere
Publishing Director: Elizabeth Bond

First published by Ebury Press in 2023

www.penguin.co.uk
www.freee-foods.co.uk

A CIP catalogue record for this book is available from the British Library

ISBN 9781529916041

Printed and bound in Italy by L.E.G.O. S.p.A

The authorized representative in the EEA is Penguin Random House
Ireland, Morrison Chambers, 32 Nassau Street, Dublin D02 YH68.